Tents, Boats and the Ones That Got Away: Outdoor Memories

Jim —
For the love of
wild places.
Tim

By Tim Mead

TENTS, BOATS AND THE ONES THAT GOT AWAY:
OUTDOOR MEMORIES

Ancient Angler Press
7124 Chapparall Ln.
Charlotte, NC 28215
www.TimMeadFishing.com
ancientanglertim@aol.com

International Standard Book Number: 978-0-9889394-1-7

Dedication

To Mom and Dad, both Nancys, and Craig.

Each, in their own way, made these tales possible.

Foreword

This series of recollections has been thirty years in the writing and a lifetime in the making. Some chapters are brand new. Some, however, were written years ago and lay a-moldering. In part, I am using them now to honor those who helped and accompanied me on these outdoor adventures. In part, I am using them because they represent tales I want to share.

Two principles, announced by earlier writers, guide these recollections. In the early pages of *Walden*, Thoreau said his book was written in the first person, "the I." He said, "I am confined to this theme by the narrowness of my experience." I, too, am so confined. These are my experiences as I recall them. The other proposition, announced by Huck Finn at the beginning of Mark Twain's description of Huck's adventures, noted in the author's *The Adventures of Tom Sawyer* is, "He told the truth, mainly." I have tried to tell the truth, mainly. I can't ask Mom or Dad for their memories. Some of the earlier writings do have their insight. Nancy Bond, my sister, has enriched some of my tales. Indeed, she said, "Some of the events he mentions I did not remember – even though I was there." Over the years, many of those who appear in these pages have offered their perspectives; I have taken them into account.

To resolve a possible confusion, two Nancys appear. One is my "little sister," now Nancy Bond. The other is my late wife, also a Nancy. In most places, the context will suffice to distinguish which Nancy is meant. Where I thought there might be confusion, I have specified.

Novelist Pat Conroy said (I'm told), "The most powerful words in English are, 'Tell me a story.'" Any skills I have as a story teller I owe to Dad. Sister Nancy recalled that wife Nancy once told her about "Meads," as Dad's recollections were called. Wife Nancy said that once she was in the family long enough and became one of the subjects of a "Mead," "that's not how that happened." Yet, it was "the truth, mainly."

Some chapters were prepared for this book. Others, in varied forms, appeared in diverse publications, including *Esox Angler, West Coast Fly Fishing, Woods-and-Water News, Midwest Outdoor Journal, Fly Fishing and Tying Journal*, and *Fish Alaska*. "Journey to Cold Mountain," Chapter 12, appeared in *Smoky Mountain Journal* and took Third Place in the Camping Division of the Outdoor Writers Association of America Excellence in Craft competition. A couple appeared on my website, www.TimMead-Fishing.com.

Several chapters suffer a paucity of pictures. At the time, I had no idea I needed pictures of Bill Yunk, Dick Jones, Johnnie Reule or others. Further, I did not have a camera. To the extent possible, I have mined the family archives for photographs. Some of the older images are not as sharp as the newer ones – better equipment now and age has taken its toll as well. I believe, however, the photos I used reflect well on the tales. So I make a note, not offer an apology. The image with Chapter 12, "Journey to Cold Mountain," is used with permission from Visit NC Smokies. The photos used in Chapter 21, "Golden Opportunity," are used with permission from good friend Jim Low and Jim retains all rights to these images.

Many other friends whose names do not appear here nonetheless have enriched my days outdoors. Lee Reeve, a high school fishing and camping buddy, contributed. Among the friends of more recent years Tim Mc-Dermott, Clyde Osborne, Banks Miller, Bill Kraft, Bill Shumaker, Gordy Johnson and Tony Garitta played significant roles.

Several have assisted in the preparation of the manuscript. Tony Garitta, a fellow outdoor writer and frequent angling companion, and Nancy Bond read the manuscript. Tony is a retired English Professor. And Nancy recalls every rule of grammar and syntax she ever learned; her children will confirm my assessment. Their constructive criticism has improved and enriched the text. Most of their suggestions I have taken. I am reminded, nonetheless, of Winston Churchill's retort when an editor told him to revise a text to eliminate sentences ending in a preposition. Churchill is alleged to have responded, "This is the sort of nonsense up with which I will not put."

Chris Madson, long time editor of the Wyoming Game and Fish Departments' award winning *Wyoming Wildlife* magazine, graciously provided an Introduction. Chris is an astute outdoorsman and a good friend. I am complimented to have his Introduction to these essays.

Gordy Johnson, as he did with my earlier book, *Quetico Adventures*, provided frequent solutions to my myriad computer problems. Though he may have thought so, he never said, "I told you how to do this earlier." Perhaps I make Gordy's life more complicated, but he makes mine easier.

Kevin Rhoades, providing the service he did with *Quetico Adventures*, prepared my manuscript for publication.

Bill Powell, Legal Counsel for the Outdoor Writers Association of America and one of the heroes of Chapter 21, and one of his associates, provided thoughts relative to copyright and trademark infringement. I am indebted to their wisdom.

– Tim Mead

Table of Contents

Introduction

I'm standing on a gravel bank with the butt of a canepole clamped under my armpit and both hands squeezing the cane, struggling to keep the tip steady. The sun dances on the water as the breeze pushes wavelets across the lake to slap the sand at my feet. A very big place it seems, almost scary, but there is a tall shadow behind me that gives me a feeling of safety.

"Watch the bobber," the voice intones, calling me back to my duty.

"Watcha bobba."

And the bobber twitches.

It may be my earliest memory.

There was a lot to be learned after that, not only the knots and tackle and boats and bait, but the patience, the optimism that must be tended and cherished like a campfire on a cold morning, that a fish will come. Those lessons were all in the future for me, but after that one bright morning, I was hooked. It happens that way, more often than not, a child barely able to walk finds himself attached to the world by hook and line.

Tim Mead was a toddler when he caught his first fish, or, more accurately, when that first fish caught him. He says he can't remember the moment, and yet, that moment helped shape the rest of his life. For nearly eight decades, it has led him across North America, from the fertile ponds and estuaries of Virginia to the lakes of Michigan's Upper Peninsula and on into the canoe wilderness of Canada's Quetico Provincial Park, the black timber of Canada and Alaska, and the crystal waters above timberline in the backcountry of the Rockies. The fascination has never faded for him; in fact, it seems to have deepened over the years, and that phenomenon leads to a question: What is it about this strange avocation that can beguile an otherwise sensible person for his entire life?

There are many answers, I suppose, possibly as many answers as there are fishermen, but I suspect that one underlying component is our connection with water. If the biologists are right, all life began in water, and all living things, even the kangaroo rats in the Sahara, depend on it for survival. Those of us who abandoned our gills and fins for the great adventure on dry land cut ourselves off from the element that gave us birth, and we now regard that cradle from the outside, unable to return for more than a few minutes, unless we resort to some technological crutch that isolates us from a real connection with water just as surely as our need to breathe air.

Except in rare places, the human eye can't penetrate more than a few inches below the surface, and even then, our view is bent, distorted, unreliable. Most of what goes on there is hidden— three-fourths of the planet pursuing its own business to its own ends beyond our knowledge. The fisherman explores this alien realm indirectly, learning by feel what he cannot see, and this sense of exploration by touch is part of what the dyed-in-the-wool angler finds so endlessly fascinating.

This intimate study of water and the life it supports eventually leads a serious fisherman to an almost subliminal understanding of the land around him. Good fishing depends on good water, and good water is a reflection of the quality of the land through which it flows. In his pursuit of good fishing, then, the fisherman gravitates to the best corners of the land we have left.

A while back, Tim and I rendezvoused in southern Montana to backpack into the Beartooth Wilderness. The stated objective of the trip was a small lake reputed to support a cooperative population of golden trout. It was only seven miles from the trailhead, but in the high country, the accessibility of a piece of water is seldom told by mileage alone. We climbed more than 3,000 vertical feet in those seven miles, and by the time our destination came into view, we had both been reminded that there is significantly less air at the elevation of 9,500 feet than there is at sea level.

We set up camp, strung up our fly rods, and walked down to the lake for the last hour or two of light. It was hard to tell where the land stopped and the water started, the water as pristine as when it had dropped out of the clouds as snow the previous winter. As we watched, a small circular bulge disturbed the surface about fifty feet out, the single ripple spreading a foot or two before it died. Then, a little closer, another bulge.

As it turned out, the lake's reputation was at least partly deserved. There were goldens alright, plenty of them, but for fish that saw open water no more than four months out of a typical year, they were a little picky about what they ate. We spent nearly two hours researching their preferences before we had enough for dinner.

Back at camp, we started the campfire, and while we waited for it to burn down to the coals for cooking, we watched the shadows creep up the sheer granite wall on the other side of the lake while we talked about the hike and the goldens and the plan for the next day. As the stars came out, the conversation wandered off to other places, other good times, fish we had lost and people we had met in the process. Finally, with the last logs burning down, we settled into a comfortable silence as the bright path of the Milky Way spread out above us and the cool night breeze slipped down from the snowfields on the surrounding peaks.

Many of the stories Tim tells in this book are like that day; they begin with the pursuit of a fish but wander out into a broader encounter with people and places he has discovered over a rich life. If, like Tim, you are a fisherman, these stories will remind you of one thing all anglers share: We are all of us bound to the world by hook and line.

– Chris Madson

Chapter 1
A Kid Starts Fishing

As is true with many anglers, I cannot remember the first time I went fishing. According to family legend, Dad took me fishing early one spring when I was scarcely three years old. He had a wooden boat he kept on Bar Lake behind the house in Arcadia, Michigan. So goes the tale, we took the boat and I caught one fat springtime crappie after another – although we called them speckled bass. Dad held the back of my life jacket, baited hooks, removed the fish, and put them on the stringer.

Me with an early stringer of pike caught at Arcadia, early 1950s.

Yet, one trip does not an angler make. Several folks played key roles in getting me started on a lifetime commitment to fishing.

Dad and Mom

Dad was instrumental in introducing me to fishing. In addition to the early times together, over the years we remained good fishing buddies. We fished together for more than 50 years. In later years we included my son, Craig.

When just a kid, I learned several key fishing lessons from Dad. The most enduring has been that all kinds of fishing should be fun. The species caught did not make any difference. Bluegills and sunfish were sought on the days they were biting. If crappie were active, we went for them. Perhaps

Dad with a smallmouth bass outside the house in Arcadia, sometime in the late 1940s.

the diverse quarry we caught was simply because I was a little guy and Dad wanted to be sure we were successful. Nonetheless, I learned from these times we did not have to catch a particular species to have a good time.

Another key lesson was that getting bait was part of going fishing. In the early years, I doubt I knew bait could be purchased. For bait, Dad and I used whatever nature provided in sufficient abundance – worms, minnows, grasshoppers, or crickets. There was a white cedar swamp just outside the little town in Michigan where I was born. The earth there was black and moist and filled with fat, blue earthworms. Though the mosquitoes in northern cedar swamps rival any in North America, and I remember the place was filled with them, I do not recall they interfered with us. Dad turned the dirt with a shovel, and I picked up the worms and dropped them in a tin can. Over the years, I cannot remember ever digging worms where they were as plentiful as they were there. Condominiums sit on a filled-in swamp now and no fathers and sons dig worms. We also seined minnows. I must have been about five years old the first time we netted minnows. We went to "the harbor," a shallow, sandy bottom, inlet between Bar Lake and Lake Michigan. Dad kept yelling instructions, the same instructions I later gave Craig. "Keep the net tight." "Keep the net close to the bottom, they'll get away." Dad explained why one side of the net had wooden floats and the other lead weights and how they helped catch the minnows. Further, I learned we could try again if we did not get enough minnows the first time. A lesson of some utility in life – try again.

By the time I was in high school, I was taller than my father. So, in tougher circumstances, like along the bank at Pickerel Lake where we seined minnows, I operated the deep end of the minnow net. Dad still urged me to "keep the net tight," even though I pointed out that the cedar limb tangled in the net came from the shore and was on his end of the net. I can remember Mom standing on the bank admonishing, "Earl, he can't go any deeper. The water is right to the top of his boots now."

We also used the seine to catch grasshoppers for bait. In late summer, Michigan, if you are not a farmer, is blessed with clouds of grasshoppers. Dad and I extended the seine and ran from one end of the yard to the other. We then dropped the net on the grass with the hoppers under the mesh. The hoppers simply waited for us to pick them off the net and drop them in the minnow bucket we used for minnows, hoppers and crickets. Easy pickins.'

Now I realize we caught crappies and yellow perch on minnows and bluegills and sunfish on worms, crickets and grasshoppers. At the time it simply seemed some species bit better on some days than other species. Dad, however, had it all figured out. We selected bait depending on his assessment of the prospects of catching different species. It was years before I discovered that.

Mom also played an important part in making me an angler. My folks kept the house near Lake Michigan after moving the family to southern Michigan. During the summer, Mom, my younger sister, and I returned while Dad finished his master's degree. Mom let me go down to the little lake with a cane pole and sit on a semi-public pier and fish. I was 50 years old before I learned she was terrified I would fall in the water and drown. She could look out the sun porch window to confirm I was still on the pier. Even if she saw me topple into the water, however, she could not have run the quarter mile quickly enough to yank me out. Further, Mom could not swim, at least not well enough to save us both. But it did not seem as frightening to me. And she never let on.

Whenever I caught fish, Mom "oohed and aahed" when I brought them back. She cooked them even though, as I discovered years later, she was concerned I had not cleaned them well enough.

One thing Mom did, though I doubt either of us knew how important a contribution it was, was to assist me in reading about fishing. Mom made a special effort to order Ted Trueblood's *The Anglers' Handbook*. I'm sure it was Mom who made certain at Christmas I received Ray Bergman's *Trout,* and *Bass Fishing* and J. Edson Leonard's *Flies*. I read and re-read these books and cherish them yet.

Most of all, my folks made it possible for me to fish. Dad took me with him, probably lots of times when he would have done better had he fished alone. When I was small, Dad always wanted, or so I presumed, to fish for little fish and lots of them. Years later, when I wanted to try more sophisticated techniques and fish for larger game, Dad wanted to fish for bass and pike with bait casting equipment. Of course, he had bait casting gear all along. Before I was born, he spent lots of time casting for bass at night.

I always had the gear I needed. Dad supplied hooks, poles, bobbers, sinkers, and line. Later he helped me select rods, reels, and lures and showed me how to use them.

Bill Yunk

Bill Yunk was a purist. Trout on dry flies. That was fishing. Anything else was done by lesser men for lesser quarry.

Uncle Bill was not really my uncle. I was born in my parent's apartment, the upper floor in Bill and Eva Yunk's home. By default they became uncle and aunt. One evening, probably when I was six or seven years old, I learned what taking trout on a dry fly was all about.

Uncle Bill, Aunt Eva and I were riding back roads, looking for deer. We crossed a bridge over a small creek, fifteen feet or so across. There were half a dozen cars parked along the road and fishermen scattered along the bank. Up and down the stream there were splashes and swirls. The hex hatch, called caddis by the Michigan locals, was on.

Aunt Eva urged Uncle Bill to go home, get his fly rod, and return. "No," he said. It would take too long, by the time he got back the hatch would be over, the best spots were already taken, and it was getting dark. In a few moments, however, Aunt Eva's urging and the purist's itch prevailed.

Uncle Bill brought me back to the creek with him. I had never seen anyone fly cast. It seemed to me, unlike the lessons Dad taught, Uncle Bill spent far too much time whirling his bait around in the air and too little with it in the water. Dad coached bait had to be left in the water long enough for fish to find it and they could not find it if it was not in the water. Further, Uncle Bill was using a little blob of feathers that would never catch a fish. I can remember thinking the other men, persons I could hear talking to one another about the fish they were catching, must be going about it differently than Uncle Bill.

In a few minutes, however, Uncle Bill muttered to me, "I've got one." A little boy, standing in tall marsh grass in the dark, I could not see what was going on. Shortly, Uncle Bill had a huge brown trout, the first I had ever seen, laid out in the grass. My recollection is that it was about two feet long and weighed several pounds, a trophy. When we got home and laid the fish in the kitchen sink, it seemed like (and still does) the most beautiful fish ever.

The next summer, though Aunt Eva died in the interim, I spent a week with Uncle Bill. He operated a mirror works for a furniture factory. Most of the day, I hung around while Uncle Bill made mirrors. We talked about baseball, particularly how the Detroit Tigers were doing and why. And we talked about trout fishing.

One evening, he took me trout fishing at Bear Creek, a tributary of the Manistee River. Bear Creek was 15 miles or so from town and a large portion of the trip was over gravel roads. Uncle Bill could remember when, with no cars in town, only week long trips by horse drawn carts to Bear Creek were worth the effort. Now, however, a trip after work was practical.

Bob Starke, one of Uncle Bill's fishing buddies and owner-operator of the furniture factory, went along. Bob, as I recall, was not a purist; it was rumored that he sometimes took big brown trout on streamers. What streamers were I did not know, but I could tell from the way Uncle Bill talked about them they were problematic ways to catch trout. A summer or two later Bob and another local angler got in some sort of bragging contest. Many mornings in the center of the meat counter in Mr. Schafer's market there were two brown trout caught by the contestants. Each weighed between five and seven pounds. Disparagingly, Uncle Bill suggested they had not been caught with dry flies.

Though I was not big enough to fly fish, I could station myself near a log jam and drop a worm in the water. Not the same as fly fishing, of course, but a way a kid could get started and certainly one of the steps toward virtue.

During the evening, a bat captured Uncle Bill's dry fly during a false cast. I had never seen a bat before. It splashed on the surface while Uncle Bill tried to get it unhooked. How he accomplished that I can't remember.

From beneath the log jam, I caught four small brook trout, the first trout of my career. Uncle Bill and Bob caught two each, so I was the "leader" for the evening. As grown men do, though I did not understand it at the time, they dragged me up to the home of the Department of Conservation officer who lived near the stream to operate the rearing ponds there. With great show, we displayed our catch. The officer was appropriately impressed with our fish, particularly the four brookies I caught. When we got in the car to head home, I was very pleased with my future as a trout fisherman.

The last time I fished with Uncle Bill I was in college. We went to Bear Creek with Dad. Uncle Bill had been in failing health for some time. Doctors told him fly fishing, at least for the time being, would be too strenuous. Later perhaps. So Uncle Bill was forced to fish with small lures, the size we called "fly rod" though they were ill-suited for use with a fly rod.

Whether any of us caught trout, I do not remember, though I could look it up in the log book I kept at the time. But I remember Uncle Bill admired one of my flies, an outsize #10 spent wing Adams. "Where did you get that fly?" he asked. "You can't get flies like that around here. Those are just what the caddis hatch calls for."

"Uncle Bill," I answered, "I tied those flies. Would you like some? Take a couple." At the time, he refused. He said he did not want to take flies out of my box to put in his. When I got home I tied up a dozen or so, the very best I could make, and sent them to him. Whether Uncle Bill ever caught any trout on those flies, I don't know. But I remember I got a letter from him thanking me. Dad told me Bill Yunk rarely wrote anyone or anything and I should be complimented to get a letter. I was.

Uncle Bill got me started as a trout fisherman. Many times on streams in Montana or Alaska or one of the other famous trout fishing spots where I was fishing I have thought, "I wish Uncle Bill could have fished here." Indeed, for a time, I was a purist, like Uncle Bill.

Dick Jones

The Detroit Tigers, in 1950, were in first place when I met Dick Jones and all was right in my world. My parents were friends with Dick Jones' parents. Even though Dick and his wife Millie were fifteen or twenty years older than I, they became special friends to my sister and me. We met in the Upper Peninsula when both sets of parents were searching sites

Dick Jones, on the left, teaching me to bait cast, summer, 1950.

for cabins (see Chapter 2, "The Cabin"). Perhaps the second day we were together, the fathers and sons went trout fishing at the Whitewash site on the Sucker River.

Dick, also a purist or nearly so, caught the then Michigan limit of 15. He had one rainbow about 15 inches long. All were caught on dry flies. Using worms and fishing under a shoreline stump, I caught four brook trout. Dad and Clair Jones, Dick's father, caught two each. All the way back to the cabin, Dick kept up a steady rat-a-tat about how the sons really beat the dads. He made me feel a full partner on the winning team.

That week, Dick started to teach me how to bait cast. Dad made home movies of Dick coaching me, then scurrying for cover as I drew the rod back as a prelude to another backlash. Dick also helped me undo the tangles. Now, every time I whip a spinnerbait under willow branches or drop a plastic worm next to a pier, I owe the first steps and encouragement to Dick Jones. Dick was a right-hander, and he taught me, a natural left-hander, how to cast right-handed. Now, however, I can cast with either hand, a major advantage that I would not have had Dick not taught me.

He also introduced me to the wonders of catching fish on artificial lures. Pike were (and still are) plentiful in the small lake near the cottage. Several times Dick took me with him as he cast for pike. Once, I remember, Dick had already rowed a hundred yards down the east side of the lake, but when I ran to the edge of the lake, he rowed back to get me.

Dick assured me pike were so common a lure dragged behind the boat would catch one. He gave me a red-and-white Bass Oreno. The next day I went out in a boat with others, Mom, sister Nancy, and probably Millie on the oars. Several times I thought I felt a jerk on the line and when we got back to the cabin I had a 14 inch pike, my first pike and my first fish on an artificial lure. In the next half dozen years I caught a lot of bass and pike on that lure. It is now retired and I would not put it in the water for anything.

Dick also taught me to fly cast. On the narrow trout streams of northern Michigan, fly casting is not so easy as it looks when expert Lefty Kreh does it on TV. The twisted course of the streams means alders are always just behind the caster. When I was in the eighth or ninth grade, the exalted status of a purist had evaded me, despite effort.

After a couple hours of frustration on Grand Marais Creek, I quit fishing and wandered down the stream to watch Dick and see how he did it. From the bluff above the water, I could see Dick flicking his fly under cedar branches, never tangling in the alders behind him. His fly landed deftly on the water rather than slapping the surface as mine did. Periodically, Dick caught a trout right before my eyes.

Dick saw me and yelled to ask what I was doing. I explained I was trying to see how it was done. I had never caught a trout on a dry fly and wanted to study someone else as I was not making much progress on my own. "Well," Dick said, "we'll fix that. There are always trout ahead of the beaver dam."

Dick positioned me knee deep in the water and said, "Stand right there." He eyed the beaver pond, the direction of my likely cast and the trees and branches behind me. With no chain saw for assistance, Dick tore through the underbrush, clearing the way for my backcast. With a little coaching I soon had my fly landing on the water like something natural. After a couple such casts, darned if something did not swirl at my fly. With more coaching on what do to then, I caught one, then another.

Dick always had time for me, even when it seemed he was wasting his. One year he agreed to take me bass fishing on opening day. Though I told everyone for months that Dick was taking me, when the day finally arrived, I overslept. Dick did not leave. He sat in the car waiting for me to appear. As before, he accommodated his schedule to mine. Mom realized, in the way I guess moms do, I was not up and about, and hustled me out.

We went to a lake west of town. Dick rowed the boat up the north side of the lake and we cast to the edge of the weeds. Just at dawn I noticed a swirl only a few feet from the boat. It took a couple of tries, but I dropped my Hula Popper in the open spot in the weeds where the swirl was. It disappeared. With some coaching from Dick, we got the bass in the boat. It was the first largemouth bass I caught on a plug.

John Reule

Johnnie Reule was the Scout Master the first few years I was a Scout. He tied some of his own flies, though I don't think he ever was as involved with tying as I became. For reasons I cannot recall, Johnnie and I became fishing buddies.

Johnnie's fishing passion was largemouth bass at night. Starting when I was in seventh grade, Dad, Johnnie and I went fishing at nearby lakes, starting after dinner and fishing until midnight. Dad or Johnnie rowed and I fished from the bow. At the time I wished I could either row or sit in the stern; the bow, it seemed, was where the "little guy" got assigned. Now, of course, I know the bow is the preferred position providing the first shot at fish.

Johnnie always wanted to go around the lake in the same direction. His casting rod, made of split bamboo, the premier material at the time, had a set in it. A set, or permanent bend, was very common among bamboo rods stored upright in a closet all winter. Johnnie fished almost exclusively with a black popper and he believed if he always "popped" his lure in an anti-set direction the set would be reduced or even eliminated.

Several of the first largemouth bass I ever caught were caught on those trips. I recall one which took a black Hula Popper over an extended weed bed. My four and a half foot steel rod bent toward the water and I heard – rather than saw – the splash as the two plus pound bass jumped. When we got home, I regaled Mom with just how I had done it. Years later, I enjoyed hearing Craig explain to his mom how, "When the fish swam left I held my rod tip to the right and when the fish swam right I held my rod tip to the left, just like Bill Dance said." I had no Bill Dance to serve as a model, but I told my mom how the trip went just as Craig did his mom.

Johnnie told Craig about one of our trips. While I was in high school I scarfed up a dilapidated wooden row boat (see Chapter 4, "Boats"). Dad helped me refurbish it, at least well enough that I could fish from it. When I was alone, the boat, only ten or twelve feet long, was fine. When two persons were in the boat, however, a pinhole somewhere on the transom was below the water line. Johnnie, and Dad too, had to suffer the indignity of watching their tackle box float and sitting with their feet in the water.

Reflections

None of these people ever became famous anglers, writers, or tv personalities widely known in the fishing community. Yet, when I showed interest in fishing, they spent time to encourage me. In turn, the encouragement led to a lifetime of adventure. Their patience made it easier when it came my turn to introduce Craig to fishing. They are all in my personal Hall of Fame.

At the time, the fish were most important. Now, the friendships are.

The cabin, shortly after it was built, Thanksgiving, mid 1950s.

Chapter 2
The Cabin

No discussion of these matters would be complete without an excursus on the cabin. It has been a key component of the Mead history for more than half a century. It appears and reappears in these tales.

In 1950, Mom and Dad took Nancy and me to the Upper Peninsula to visit the Joneses. They were staying at a cabin on Carpenter Lake. Carpenter Lake is a little more than a mile off M77 between Seney and Grand Marais. At the time, M77 was a gravel road. A not very good gravel road.

The Shaws had purchased a large tract around the lake and were seeking to sell off 40 acre sections. The Joneses purchased a 40 on the southwest corner of the lake and hoped my folks would buy another 40. Though I do not recall specifically, I suspect the Joneses hoped the Meads would purchase the adjacent 40. Instead, Dad bought 80 acres across the lake. The property did not have lake frontage. I can remember wishing our property was adjacent to the Shaws, but Dad did not want property part of which was under the lake. Dad did get a one rod right of way to the lake at the east side of the Shaw 40 acres. The right of way shows on county property records. We have never had to claim it as we have always had good relations with lake front property owners.

Floyd Tester owned the saw mill near the highway. He built the Shaw's cabin and the Jones's cabin. In 1952 he built our cabin. Dad could have built the cabin himself, but he thought the cabin would be better secured had it been built by a local who could watch it. We would not be there all the time. The original building was 24 feet by 18 feet.

Unlike the other cabins Floyd Tester built, our cabin had a loft. Nancy and I had our rooms in the loft, though they were not very private and I had to go through Nancy's end of the loft to get to my end. There was no electricity. Still there is no electricity. A few years before Dad died he got a letter from other property owners near the lake suggesting we join a consortium seeking electricity. Dad, Nancy and I considered the matter, none wishing to close off discussion. Finally, one of us said, "Part of what I like about the cabin is there is no electricity." The other two rapidly agreed. So I drafted a letter in response to the proposal saying we were not interested.

There are two generators at the cabin, so if we want power, we can get it. Mom liked to watch television, so Dad rigged an antenna in the loft and Mom could watch the Tigers. Reception was, however, problematic. Nancy and Holton, I think, use the small generator. In the last couple of years, I have fired it up as well. Several years ago when I tore off rotted sheeting and replaced it and later when I replaced a window, I used the big generator. Power is nice.

In the summer of 1954, Dad and I added a room to the cabin. By that time, I had worked with Dad for several years. We knocked off part of the front of the original building and built a 14 feet by 10 feet room still called "The Addition." While we were putting up the rafters, Dad was on the roof of the original cabin and I nailed the first set of rafters to the plate. Once it was secured, I headed around the plate to fasten the other end. Dad asked, "Aren't you going to do something about the blood?" In eagerness to fasten the rafters, I mashed my thumb. I trailed blood all the way. I suspect the stains are still there if there was someone to climb up to investigate.

Dad built a large stand alone closet at home. It held our clothes on one side and on the rear there were hooks to hold jackets, waders, whatever seemed most suitable. Many years later, when we were no longer using the closet, Nancy wanted to discard it. I said it was too important to the cabin history, so we put it in the pole barn (more about the pole barn later). After a couple of years in the pole barn, I acquiesced. Nancy and Holton took the closet to the highway and someone claimed it.

During the summer we built the addition, Dad and I also built a cabin for the Curtis's across the lake. The Curtis's and Jones's shared ownership of the 40 acres. I can remember Dad asking if the selected site was where the cabin should be built. He thought a surveyor should run the property lines. He was assured, the property line is "over there" and the site selected was where the cabin should be. In 1961 a surveyor found the Curtis's cabin was not built on property they owned, and they lost it.

"August 7, 1954. Mom and Nan left today. Dad and Tim felt lonely! Tim caught 2 pike and Dad and Tim one porky."

The brief entry above in the log Mom kept scarcely covers it. Until a few years ago I had forgotten Mom kept a daily log of what went on at the cabin. Forgotten to the extent I did not recall I made the entry above. Poor reporting, in my case.

Summer of 1954 in the UP was marked by sparse rain. Favorite trout streams were low. Bears were common at the Grand Marais bear dump. Raccoons and porcupines foraged widely. Near the cabin, in particular, raccoons and porkies were a pest. Several times raccoons climbed the shutter leaning against the cabin to peer in at fish cooking on the stove.

Though we chased porkies with sticks, yelled imprecations at them, and tried whatever we could to keep them away, they were relentless. Food was scarce in the woods. Cardboard boxes left outside were chewed to shreds. Canoe paddles were gnawed to uselessness. Damage done to the outhouse led Dad to get a hasp and lock the door.

Dad issued threats, gradually increasing in intensity, against the invading porkies. Finally, Dad said, "The next porky that comes around the cabin, I'm going to kill him and eat him."

A few days later, Dad and I were finishing the outside to the addition on our cabin. Dad was nailing log slabs to the sheeting. I rigged up a table where I was cleaning the slabs with a spoke shave. It was hot and scarcely a breath of air moved in the forest.

I thought I heard rustling in the woods. I stopped shaving the slab and listened. More rustling. Something was moving in the underbrush. I yelled at Dad to stop pounding. He did and the rustling stopped. "What's the matter?" he asked.

"Nothing," I answered. "Go ahead." When Dad started pounding, I heard the rustling again. I dropped my spoke shave and headed in the direction of the noise. Within a few yards I came to a huge porcupine waddling, as fast as he could, away from the cabin. "Porky, Dad," I yelled, "there's a porky right here."

I ran beyond the escaping culprit. He came over a small hump, saw me, and turned back toward the cabin. Big mistake. He met Dad. Dad whacked the porky in the head several times. The porky was dead. Dad said, "When I came around the edge of the cabin, I saw your mother's mop. So I grabbed it. We'll have to get her a new one."

Dad planned to make good on the threat to eat the porky. With due care, he took the carcass into the cabin to skin it. When Nancy read this, she said, "Mom would have croaked if she knew you did that inside." I resumed shaving the bark off slabs. Periodically I stuck my head in for an update on Dad's progress. He started gingerly at the abdomen and finally got the critter skinned. At least an hour was consumed as Dad cut lumps of pungent fat from the porky's body. Dad said, "Of all the coons, deer, rabbits I've ever cleaned, this is the greasiest animal I ever dealt with." Dad put the dressed meat in the refrigerator for dinner tomorrow.

About noon, Dad quit work on the addition and went inside to cook the porky. From time-to-time, I checked on Dad's activity. He was parboiling the meat, skimming great gobs of fat from simmering water. He told me he changed the water several times.

Early in the evening, Dad called me in to dinner. In addition to boiled potatoes and some sort of vegetable, pieces of fried porcupine were on a serving platter. The meat was black. Not dark like coon or duck. Black. Its flavor was strong and coarse, a lot like a hemlock twig. And it was tough, hard to chew and hard to swallow. We each ate a couple of small pieces, mostly to say we had done it. Then we threw the rest away.

But the porky was not finished with us.

The next day we went trout fishing. We hiked to a stream about a mile from the cabin. On our way back, Dad said he had to stop, take off his waders, and "see a man about a dog" in the woods. "We haven't got far to go, Dad, we'll walk faster." So we picked up the pace, nearly running along an old road bed.

We went another hundred yards and Dad said, "I'm not going to make it. I've got to stop."

"No problem," I told him, "I know a deer trail from here that comes out right at the cabin. Follow me." Snaking my way, fly rod and all, along the trail, I started running toward the cabin. As I entered the clearing around the cabin, Dad stopped running. "Don't stop now," I admonished.

Dad said, "Too late." With no water pressure and no hose, it's very difficult to clean the inside of waders.

We were sufficiently recovered the next day to drive a few miles to another stream. Shortly after I entered the water, I could tell I reached the point Dad had been a day earlier. As I clambered out of the water, I chucked my creel over a tree limb, my jacket over another, tugged off my waders, and backed into a thicket of nettles.

Would another method of preparing the porcupine produced better results? Don't know. We did not have access to subtle marinades or a slow-cook pot. Dad did what he thought best. But the porky got revenge.

Sometime in the 1950s male black bears marked the cabin with huge claw scratches on the corners. These scratches served two functions. They told other males, "I'm here and I'm the toughest dude in the neighborhood. Don't mess with me." And to the females, "I'm here and I'm the toughest dude in the neighborhood. Stick with me." As we have replaced the original slabs on the cabin, we have retained the scratched corners of the cabin.

In the early years, Dad and I caught brook trout in the beaver ponds near the cabin. The East Fork of Carpenter Creek runs right by the cabin. A quarter mile to the south the West Fork comes to join the East Fork. There was a large pond there. Many mornings, Dad and I wandered to the pond, caught a breakfast portion of trout and brought them to the cabin as Mom and Nancy roused out for breakfast. At some time in the mid-1960s, poachers dynamited the dams to harvest the beaver pelts. Only in the last decade did beavers recolonize Carpenter Creek and develop ponds from the lake to the northern edge of our property. Yet, in spring 2016 the new dams had been breached. What happened to the beavers, I don't know.

The cabin, after the Addition was put on.

Dad replaced the original kitchen cabinets, really just shelves with old kitchen towels hanging over the openings, in 1989 with those he built in his shop in Springport and installed as units. These are nice, professionally done, with nooks for nick-knacks on the sides, doors with small pine tree outlines, drawers that work.

No power, no pump. We still draw water by hand. The original pump is still in place, though the leather has to be changed every year or so. Doubtless leathers would last longer were they kept wet rather than dry out after a month or two of use. Each time we go to the cabin, the pump has to be primed to draw water from the well. In 1996 Phil Lonsbury and I prevailed on Dad to allow us to pull the well pipe and replace the point. Dad was concerned we would not be able to drive the new point into the exposed shaft. Phil told Dad to go to Newberry and buy a new point and said when he got back we would have the pipe out and ready to put the new point on. And it worked just like that.

That same summer, Dad, Phil and I insulated the lower level of the original cabin, paneled the wall with tongue and groove white pine and sealed the ceiling with oriented strand board. We installed a new insulated window facing the creek. These changes made the cabin cooler in the summer and snugger in the winter. On his own, Dad made and installed a long bookcase for under the window.

Dad, as folks who knew him can surmise, needed a place for his tools. He added a small shed to the addition in 1982. Later, Dad, Nancy and I converted the shed to a bed room which could sleep four in a pinch.

Dad's tools, in turn, needed a place. Dad built a tool shed near the southeast corner of the expanded cabin. Mom wrote in her log for August 1989, "Earl worked all day on his building," and, "Earl is out working—I hope he does not get too hot." Early in its history, half of the shed sheltered fire wood. Later Dad closed that section and it was used only as a tool and work shed. Craig and I were at the cabin when Dad was on the roof of the new shed laying shingles. Craig said, "I don't think Grandpa should be up there." I asked Craig if he was willing to climb the ladder and tell his grandfather to get down. When he demurred, I suggested we better get up there and help finish the roof.

The cabin, as it looks today, February, 2007.

Dad also added a red steel pole barn to house boats, bicycles, canoes, picnic tables and other miscellaneous gear. It seemed pretty big at the time, but in use we have to take care closing the door when we leave as the accumulated stuff approaches too much.

Nancy Bond wanted a shower. For a number of years I used a Sun Shower©. Take care – if it is in the sunlight too long, water from a Sun Shower© reaches scalding temperatures. I hang the device on a hook near the roof of the pole barn and shower there. Yet, this approach was not what Nancy wanted. Holton designed and Herm Tester built an enclosed outdoor shower facility and erected it behind the tool shed. Confession: Nancy's shower is pretty neat.

The outhouse is the only other building. It is a two-holer. Most of the building is original, constructed by Floyd Tester. When I told Dad, about 15 years ago, we needed to dig a new pit, he said we never had a pit. He pointed out the lower portion of the rear of the outhouse was removable and whatever was there could be taken out and buried in the forest. Sure enough. When I cleaned it out, however, all there was to extract was a wheel barrow load of gray dust. I replaced the lower board a couple of years ago.

There is a sign announcing the site belongs to "Mead." Dad built it early on. A couple of years before Dad died, he and I took the back panel off. It was made of plywood and moisture over the years separated the layers. We took the letters and numbers off the board, made a new one, and Nancy Bond and I installed it.

For a number of years I did not visit the cabin much. Graduate school, new job, getting married – all took priority. Once Craig was born and able to travel, Mom and Dad invited Craig to come to the cabin, starting in 1982. As I had many years before, Craig was introduced to the small pike in Carpenter Lake. By the time Craig was 15, he and I came to the cabin almost every summer to spend time with my folks.

Nancy Bond's kids have also been frequent visitors to the cabin. Steve Bond spent his fourth birthday at the cabin. In 2016, Steve's and Sarah's twins celebrated their fourth birthday at the cabin. The twins had such a good time, Finn's face was scrunched and near tears as his dad drove toward home.

The interior is jammed with family mementos from the beginning. The lemonwood bow Dad made in one of his undergraduate classes at Western Michigan Normal School (now Western Michigan University). Antlers from the deer Dad killed in Sweet's Ravine before I was born. An impressionistic cedar silhouette Dad made of some trophy yellow perch Mom, Nancy and Dad caught (I baited hooks, unhooked caught perch, put fish on the stringer – by the time I had one done another was swinging my way). Souvenirs of travels across North America. Pictures of family, now into the fourth generation.

And so it has been, for more than half a century. The cabin and things that have happened while we were there have been a central part of our family history. When Holton Bond, sister Nancy's husband, scanned Mom's scrap book, he included a note Dad wrote when he was at the cabin alone. Dad said, "Over the years at the cabin I began to realize that it has been one of the things that helped keep the family to be together. A family has to give and take to make a complete family. And I think back and I think the Mead family has had a good life, And the cabin has helped out." It's just a building with some out structures, I know. Yet somehow it has been a crucial glue which helped us stay a family.

What a big fish looks like just before it gets away.

Chapter 3
Big Ones that Got Away

Among sceptics, even among many anglers, it is a cliché that the big ones always get away. They don't, of course. There are enough wall mounts and photos around to demonstrate that some of them get caught. Big ones that get away, however, make for great fishing stories. Stories that need to be repeated to propitiate the gods of both fishing and conversation.

Of the big ones that got away, perhaps the most memorable in my angling career, was an enormous pike. During the summer of 1948, Mom and Dad loaded the entire family in the two-tone Oldsmobile, a new car long anticipated at the end of World War II, and headed north. We wandered into Ontario north of the Soo to the point where the road ended at the Montreal River. Then we returned to the Upper Peninsula, traveling east to west.

Probably as a money saving device, but I thought it a great way to live, we camped, moving from campground to campground. Eventually we were at the east end of the Dead River Storage Basin, west of Marquette. There was a campground there and we pitched our tent. Dad rented a small boat, somewhere, and we went fishing.

I could not cast. We had no live bait. We trolled, Dad rowing while I sat in back. Dad doubtless had some idea of where we were going and how we were fishing, but for me it was just fishing. As dark approached, we were on the south side of the reservoir moving back toward the campground. My recollection is the campground was not in sight but we then rounded a point and could see the tent. Dad's steel rod, which I still have, was resting on the floor of the boat with the tip extending over the side.

Dad was fishing with a Heddon Dowagiac, a heavy lure about six inches long with a small spinner at each end. I did not know the name of the lure then, but I recall Dad had two, one brown and one blue. Which one he was using at the time I do not remember.

With no signal that I noticed, Dad suddenly picked up his rod and said he had a fish. But I could not see any fish and he did not bring it in. Dad kept talking about what a big fish it was, and I can remember some folks on the bank yelling to us (or at us).

Then Dad had the fish right next to the boat. He must have played it well because I can remember the fish motionless in the water with the lure resting along its face. Dad said it was a pike. I had never seen a pike. Its eyes looked up at us; years later when I learned the word malevolent, I knew what it meant.

How big a fish was it? Its tail was beside me at the stern and its head was adjacent to Dad in the middle of the boat. Dad said it was "as long as a canoe paddle," about four feet. Its back was broad and green, almost black.

I must have been pretty excited. Dad had to yell at me to calm down. While he was trying to land the fish of a lifetime, with no net, he also had to deal with a little guy going wild. Years later, when Craig was small and the cycle came round, I had to do the same thing. Dad says I proposed hitting the fish with an oar and tried to get one of the oars out of the oarlock. Later Dad admonished me he would not be able to take me fishing if I was a threat to myself (and possibly him as well).

Suddenly, the lure dropped away from the huge pike's jaw, and the fish simply disappeared below the surface. Gone. The big fish had gotten away.

Years later, after reading a draft of this chapter, Mom apologized to me. She said she "shushed" me, though I do not recall that part, when I came running into camp to tell her about the big fish that got away because Nancy – my little sister – had just gone to sleep.

Eight years later, it was my turn. By that time I was keeping a log, so I know it was June 11, 1956. I had just graduated from high school. A few days earlier, Mom, Nancy, Dad and I caught a big mess of large perch and I had a limit of five pike fishing at Pickerel Lake, a small lake a few miles from the cabin. We fished from the canoe, Dad in the stern, me in the bow and Mom and Nancy seated on the floor between us. Nancy recalled it was hard to lift fish over the gunnels while sitting on the bottom of the canoe. I caught my pike on smaller perch they caught as I spent most of my day taking perch off hooks, rebaiting hooks with minnows Dad and I seined along the shore, putting caught fish on a stringer, and other administrative chores associated with a day when fish are biting faster than can be easily accommodated. The pike I caught were by-products of the perch fishing.

My notes indicate Dad and I waited for an early morning shower to pass a few days later and then returned to Pickerel Lake. We got some minnows for bait, paddled across the lake and anchored in a likely spot. The plan was to catch another mess of big perch, with pike on the side. Within moments, we were doing so. Our strategy had been to fish for pike with four or five inch perch as bait, but we could not catch any that small. We had to use seven and eight inch fish.

Dad and I had a rule. Whoever first got a pike to take a perch had priority. In order to avoid getting lines tangled, the second person was to bring his bait close to the canoe until the first pike was landed or got away. Dad's perch was fifty or sixty feet from the canoe in one direction and mine a comparable distance in another. My bobber was a few feet from a small patch of lily pads. We were fishing two or three feet deep below round cork bobbers about two inches across. As had happened several times before, Dad's bobber began the dance suggesting a pike was taking the bait. I reeled my line in about ten feet from the canoe and left the perch in the water to keep it alive.

What happened to Dad's fish, I do not remember. But while he was dealing with it, my bobber popped below the surface and started away from the canoe, fast. "I've got one too, Dad, but I'll pull it away from him." And I did. I meant to jerk the perch out of the pike's mouth, so I gave a pretty good yank. My nearly new fiberglass rod bent into a U and the canoe rocked.

Line peeled off my reel as the fish headed rapidly toward the main part of the lake. Sixty or 70 feet from the canoe, the pike turned right and doubled back along the shore. As it did, I regained some line. Rapidly the fish swam along the shore, from our left to right. Water where the fish was moving was shallow enough a distinct wake appeared and the line made a hissing noise as it sliced through the water. Dad and I both knew I had hooked a big pike, bigger than any we caught before. Now I was losing line again. The pike swam toward deeper water. Somehow I got turned around and prevented the line from tangling on Dad or the stern. Dad probably lifted the line over his head and canoe.

A little slower, but still very deliberately and without much influence from me, the fish came right toward the canoe and a few feet from the side. It was huge. Typical of Pickerel Lake pike, it was brown on the back and the yellow spots stood out like bright pennies. It was at least 15 pounds, perhaps 20, and bigger than any pike I ever caught by a factor of four or five.

Then I panicked. When the monster pike was only a few feet from me, I clamped my thumb on the spool and froze. Though I had a state-of-the-art South Bend reel, a reel I still have but no longer use, there was no adjustable drag as there is on reels made after the mid-1970s. My entire judgment had to be in my thumb and my thumb failed me. The pike surged away from the canoe and the brand new 15 pound test line popped. The rod went limp and so did my heart.

What constitutes a big fish, of course, is relative. To a fresh high school graduate, it must be an objectively large fish. To a little kid, however, just bigger than usual is big.

My fishing career started at Bar Lake near Arcadia. Dad and I fished for bluegills, crappie (we called them calico bass), perch, or whatever else we could catch. We always fished with cane poles and bobbers – still fishing. Now I know that was the only way a kid could fish effectively. Dad fished that way because I could fish too. Those were good times.

Most of the time we fished along slabs of wood, called edgings. As the furniture factory in Arcadia sawed logs, the discarded slabs were piled along the side of the lake where eventually they sank, making great fish cover. At one spot there was a cove in the wooden pieces Dad called "the slip." It was 60 or 70 feet long and 30 feet wide at the mouth. On the deepest side, the water was plenty deep, perhaps 15 feet.

I was about four years old and Dad and I were fishing in the slip. If the fish were not pulling my bobber under every few minutes, my mind wandered to other matters. Sometimes I tapped the float with the pole; after all, that's the idea, to get it to dip below the surface. Other times, I just ignored the whole thing. I tossed my bait over toward the wooden cover. Nothing happened, and my bobber drifted out of sight around the stern. At some point, I began to look for my bobber, but it was gone. As I had been taught, I pulled. The cane pole bent, so I pulled harder. The fish pulled and I pulled back. Soon I could see an open mouth, lined in brilliant white – all these years and I still see it.

Dad could tell his earlier instructions about lifting fish into the boat and not dallying around was inappropriate in this case. In the time honored language of anglers, he yelled, "Don't horse him, don't horse him." And in the time honored tradition of kids receiving instruction, I applied Dad's advice to the fullest. I learned the corollary of "don't horse him" is "keep a tight line." The fish was gone. Dad thought it was a largemouth bass about three pounds. Years would pass before I caught one that big.

Sometimes big fish get away because the gear is not matched to the fish. When we lived in York County, Pennsylvania, I lost two muskies in the Susquehanna River because my gear was not adequate. Someone told me the area around the Pennsylvania Turnpike Bridge was great for small-mouth bass. According to my source, the perch colored Bass Oreno was the lure which would catch them. I bought two.

I had never fished the Susquehanna, but I made my way through New Cumberland in the direction of the Turnpike Bridge. I found a spot to park under the bridge, crossed the railroad tracks, clambered down the hill, and waded into the water. A hundred yards or so, a large rock broached the surface, breaking the current, and creating eddies and still spots.

For a decade, I had done very little fishing. Graduate school, getting married, and finding jobs had taken lots of time. For Christmas, 1973 I asked for new spinning gear, suitable for trout and smallmouth bass. Mom and Dad obliged and I put eight pound test line on the closed-face Shakespeare reel. With that gear, I made my way, casting diagonally across the current. Without warning, about 20 feet upstream of the rock there was a huge boil in the water and my tiny Bass Oren disappeared. Fish on! Past the rock she went and toward the airport on the far side of the River. When the big fish had well over 50 yards of line out, I decided to do something to stop her. I tightened the drag a little and the line popped.

After several minutes sitting on the bank, heart pounding, I recovered enough to tie on the second Bass Oreno. Though I caught several fine smallmouth, my thoughts remained with the big muskie.

A couple of days later, reinforced with new line and a couple more Bass Orenos, I returned to the Turnpike Bridge. The smallies were still active, and I caught some downstream from the bridge. Filled with anticipation, I approached the rock. I made numerous casts from different angles which brought the lure past the spot where I hooked the big fish. She was not there.

Disappointed the big fish was not home or not striking, I moved below the obstruction. I was making short casts into the swirling water. When the lure was in the center of the largest eddy, there was another boil. In the days since I lost the big fish, I resolved no freshwater fish could run off 150 yards of line and I would let the fish run. Did not work.

The oldest and wisest of anglers say, no matter how big the fish and light the gear, unless the line tangles around a rock, limb or other obstruction, a fish should never break your line. Perhaps, but I was outmatched by these two Susquehanna River muskies. I promised Hal Alexander, my neighbor, I would catch a Susquehanna River muskie, but I never did. Unfortunately, fishing in the Susquehanna has fallen on evil days. Pollution has ruined a fine fishery. May it recover.

Leon Sagaloff, a trout guide and friend in Montana, reminded me sometimes a fish is too large and powerful for the occasion. We were fishing on the Beaverhead River near Dillon. Leon was sitting under the alders as I drifted nymphs. After I caught a 20 inch rainbow I was feeling pretty good. I was standing, ankle deep, on a boulder. After several drifts through a seam to my right, I dropped my flies near my feet where the swirling current swept them rapidly away. Finally, certain there were trout in the slack current close to where I stood, I lowered the leader almost straight down. The flies sank as expected but the strike indicator lay on the water without moving. "Darn," I thought, "now I'm hung." I lifted my rod tip to free the flies and away they went, downstream, fast. Big trout. "Leon," I yelled, "I've got a big one."

In the few seconds we had, I explained to Leon I could not follow the fish as the current was too swift and the water too deep. By now the trout was 60 or 70 feet downstream, wallowing on the surface. When the fish started moving powerfully away, Leon said, "You can't just let her run. You've got to make her pay." I put a little more pressure on the spool and the leader parted. Several years later, Leon recalled what happened. "That fish just over-powered you. You didn't do anything wrong," he said.

No doubt the most publicly noticed big fish that ever got away, at least for me, was a trophy pike on Phelps Lake in Saskatchewan. I was fishing out of Wolf Bay Lodge with Pete Maina. Pete was at Wolf Bay as a result of contacts I initiated between Pete and Brent Osika, owner of the Lodge. The idea was to catch big pike on a fly rod for Pete's nationally distributed TV show, "The Next Bite." There was lots of film already shot, plenty to fill the 20 some minutes of Pete's show. It was late in the evening and Pete was fishing with bait casting gear into a narrow slot with a reputation for yielding trophies.

I looked into the water about 20 feet from the boat and there was a monster pike, well into the mid-40 inch range, just resting near the bottom. I flipped my fly beyond the fish, stripped it in front of her, and it disappeared. One hard strip to set the hook and the battle was on. It took eight or 10 minutes to bring the big fish close enough to the boat for Pete to lean down with the cradle and I led the pike into it. Success.

After I put the rod down and unhooked the fish, the camera man wanted me to lift the fish out of the water and hold it for a "grip and grin." Over the years I have lifted dozens, perhaps more, pike over 40 inches with a hand under the gill covers. I grabbed the fish, told Pete I had her, and Pete lowered the cradle. The big pike flopped, hard, slid out of my hand and slowly swam away. The big fish that got away, but it made great images for Pete's show.

So, it's true. Big fish do get away. They break line. Get tangled in obstructions. Over-power gear. Angler error. All play a part in the tales of broken hearts. Izaak Walton, in *The Compleat Angler*, on the Fourth Day, advised his pupil, "Nay, the Trout is not lost; for pray take notice, no man can lose what he never had."

Chapter 4
Boats, Canoes and Kayaks

My first boat was a salvage job. For several years a wooden boat lay, bottom side up, in the yard across Pearl Street from the high school. It had been abandoned when Mrs. Farmer, the Home Ec teacher, left Springport High School. She and Bill, her husband, lived in the small house and Bill did not take the boat when they headed out.

After an event at school, I asked Mr. Schwei, the School Superintendent who lived in the house, what he was going to do with the boat, now covered with several inches of snow. He said, "Saturday morning I'm going out there with a sledge hammer and smash it all to pieces. If someone comes and gets it before then, they will save me the trouble."

Though dubious, Dad helped me dig the boat out of the snow, load it in the back of the Chevy pickup, take it home, and carry it into the basement. It was a sorry sight. Perhaps ten feet long and three feet wide at the stern, it was not very large. Several of the boards on the bottom were rotted. One side was split. The transom was shot. The bow needed to be replaced. Dad wondered whether it was worth the effort. But it was my boat and I wanted to go fishing. So, Dad helped me replace the floor boards, put in a new transom, install new seats. When we got it put back together, we calked all the joints. Given the quality of the remaining wood and the problematic character of the enterprise, Dad got out the oldest, thickest paint he could find (understand, in those days at our house the supply of old paint, nails, screws, bolts and other materials was without apparent limit) and told me to paint the boat. He said, "Maybe this thick paint will fill all the holes." If I went fishing alone, all the holes were patched. When someone went with me, however, there was a leak halfway up the transom and after an hour or two we had water up to our ankles.

When summer came, I took the boat to Clark Lake, one of the Gang Lakes west of Springport. A farmer, for a small fee, let people use his lane to access the lake. There were several pipes driven into the ground near the lake and I took my boat to the lake and chained it to one of the pipes. Once, after fishing late into the evening, I got the truck stuck in the muddy lane a few feet from the gate. I had to go to the farmhouse and rouse the farmer to pull me out of the goo. Over the years I suspect this happened often, but he did not complain – at least to me.

And I caught fish. Usually I fished alone. My senior year in high school I made several trips in autumn after classes. Fishing near the weeds or over the top of them, I caught four, four pound largemouth bass – big fish for Michigan – and earned a reputation as a big fish angler.

Dad went with me a number of times and sometimes Johnnie Reule accompanied me. Nancy, my sister, caught a smallmouth bass trolling one evening, the only smallmouth I saw in southern Michigan. Once when a largemouth jumped and tossed my popper a few feet from the boat Nancy exclaimed, "Just like on the cover of *Sports Afield*."

What became of the boat after I left home for college, I don't know.

Dad made several boats. The first I recall was rectangular, perhaps eight feet by four feet, just the size of a single sheet of plywood. It had seats across the stern and the bow, while not technically a seat, could accommodate a couple of fannies. About a quarter of the way toward the bow, there was a well open to the water. The well was to accommodate Dad's outboard motor, a Sears five horsepower with the gas tank circling the cowling. Once fishing Bar Lake near Arcadia, a wave lifted the boat and then dropped the well over a piling. Of course, we could not get out to let the boat float off the obstruction. Dad stuck his foot through the well, pushed on the piling as he lifted the boat. At some delay, we floated off.

Eventually, the boat ended up at the cabin in the UP. When our stay ended, we carried it inside to keep it out of the weather. For several years it was the only boat at the cabin. Somewhere I read, probably from Ted Trueblood (oh for the days when outdoor writers really knew), pike anglers did not need wire leaders. Rather, a length of monofilament could be used as a leader. Monofilament, according to my source, could be dyed to make it less visible to fish. I took a spool of monofilament and dyed it pale brown to match the tannin-stained lake and used it to make leaders. Fishing with Nancy I tested the visibility of my leaders. I cast to one side of the boat, swung my rod to the other and began to retrieve so the line was directly under the well. With a jacket or some other covering over her head, Nancy peered through the well as my line passed. Suddenly she yelled, "Your line broke, it's gone." No, the dyed monofilament worked.

When she read a draft of this chapter, Nancy reminded me of something I had forgotten. She said, "Remember you used to drop the anchor through the well in the middle of the boat. A couple of times when a pike got tangled in the anchor rope, you walked around the top of the boat on the edge opposite the way the fish went. That boat was so stable, you couldn't tip it over. Maybe that's why Mom and Dad let two kids go out in the boat alone." The part Nancy left out is, one year I bought her a life jacket for Christmas (what big brother buys his little sister a life jacket?) after asking our folks if they would let me take her out in the boat if she had one.

June 27, 1954, according to Mom's log, friends from Springport showed up at the Jones' cabin across the lake. Were they invited or did they just appear? I have a lingering suspicion it was the latter. The Jones did not have extra space, so the adults and the smallest child stayed in the travel trailer the friends brought to the Jones' cabin. Sam and Elizabeth stayed at our cabin. Sam was a couple of years ahead of me in high school and Elizabeth was a year behind. Turned out, I took Sam fishing several days in the rectangular boat.

Toward the southwest corner of Carpenter Lake there was a log in water. Based on something I read in some magazine, I figured I could catch pike on a topwater lure. Near the log I had a strike on a Heddon Crazy Crawler from what I was sure was a big fish. I still have the lure and never caught a single fish on it. On one of our revolutions of the lake, Sam hooked a pike near the log. Then he reached down to slap a mosquito on his leg and the fish was gone. I was disappointed, no offended, that I took Sam to a spot where he could catch a big fish – a couple of pounds? – and he let it get away.

When we sold the property in Springport, the boat was in the loft in the barn. It did not get taken at the auction, so I gave it to Phil Lonsbery.

Dad built another boat about the same time. It was longer, wider and shaped like a boat. It was hard to row, at least for me because it was so big, perhaps 16 feet, and wide. It was stable and I could stand anywhere I wanted to cast. One thing I remember about the boat was a day I was fishing at Carpenter Lake and two teenage girls rowed all over the lake wanting to talk to me. I was either finishing high school or early in college. Once I rowed as rapidly as I could from one end of the lake to the other to get away from them but they followed me. Dad thought the episode pretty funny.

For many years, I did not have a boat. Over time, the idea of what a fishing boat looked like, at least at the top end, changed. *Bassmaster* and other magazines were filled with images of new-fangled bass boats. Those images were burning a hole in my psyche. In 1978 I answered an ad in *Bassmaster* for a kit to build my own bass boat. I was enticed, also, by the assurance I could become a field rep for the company and soon make enough to recover my investment. That prospect never materialized.

Late one afternoon, I got a phone call at work. A female voice asked if I was the person who ordered a bass boat and would I be home in the early morning. The voice said, "We're in Pittsburgh and we can be in Virginia by 6:00." I assured her we would be ready. To myself I thought, "So the truck driver travels with his girlfriend."

Sure enough, the next morning an 18-wheeler with several boat hulls came down our twisty-turny suburban street. A tiny woman jumped out of the passenger side and came toward the house. She asked if this was the right place and I assured her it was. I wanted the boat unloaded as close to one side of the two car garage as possible. The young woman went out to the street and started waving her arms. The driver put the rig right where it needed to be. And got out. Another tiny young woman. The driver and her cohort were in their mid-20s, not more than five feet and a couple of inches tall, and neither weighed more than 125 pounds. But they could drive a monster truck and unload boat kits.

The kit itself was of three parts – a hull, a deck, and a console. Assembling them into a boat was not a simple task. For one thing, there were errors and inconsistencies in the instruction manual. Had I not experienced building and the lessons from it with Dad, I could never have completed the task. The most important error concerned the ribbing on the hull and under the deck. The ribbing was parallel to the center where the hull was depressed to allow water in the boat to run to the stern, with other members crossing the width of the hull. These pieces were to be secured in place with fiberglass mesh and liquid resin. Carefully, I measured the pieces of plywood for the ribbing, making sure the pieces I cut matched the template provided.

Before I fastened the pieces to the hull, I put the deck over the hull with the ribbing and floor in place. I went across the street to get Fred Rudder to help me. When we set the deck over the hull it did not fit. The ribbing was about half an inch too high. Fred asked if I wanted to lift the deck off and I said, "No, I want it to sit here while I try to figure out what's wrong." Fred went home. For an hour or so, I contemplated what I saw, tried to wiggle the deck to get it to settle in place, contemplated some more. Finally, I asked Fred to help again and we lifted the deck off the hull. I sawed half an inch off the ribbing before fastening it in place. Had I fiberglassed those pieces as originally created, correcting the error would have been next to impossible.

Over the 60 or so hours it took to complete the boat, I had help. Mom and Dad came for Thanksgiving and Dad helped for two days. With his time and expertise, the project went much faster. Jere Richardson, Jr., who lived next door, was 11 years old and he came eagerly each time I needed someone to hold a piece, steady something, or do another task an enthusiastic boy could do. Jere was particularly helpful when something had to be done under the front deck as he could slide in the opening better than I. Several years later I learned Jere had been grounded during the time the boat was under construction and he was only permitted to leave the house to help me. Craig, only four, also helped. When Dad and I put down the carpet, we had Craig lay on it to hold it in place while the cement hardened.

The kit included a 35 horsepower Evinrude engine. It did not include the connectors like a gas line, steering cable or wheel, or bolts to hold the engine in place. On my lunch hour, I hiked to the waterfront in D. C. and purchased the necessary parts. Nor did it include a trolling motor, so I purchased a Minn-Kota and installed it. In the spring of 1979 the boat was finished. I took Jere and Craig to a boat ramp on the Potomac River a short distance from the airport. When I dropped the trolling motor into the water and moved us away from the bank, Jere said, "This is cool."

Craig now has the boat. Over time, the carpet and the plywood portions of the deck needed to be replaced. Craig helped me do that. He is replacing them again, along with the ribbing under the deck.

Lots of good times in that boat. Dad and I, sometimes with Craig, fished Currituck Sound when it was one of the top largemouth spots in the country. Once at Kitty Hawk Bay off the Sound I realized Craig did not have his rod. I said, "You just dropped your rod, didn't you?" He said, "Yes." I tossed a marker right there. With the trolling motor I moved upwind and anchored. I took off my shoes, socks and pants. I slid over the side of the boat and scuffed along the bottom. I found something with my feet and lifted Craig's gear and we continued fishing.

When we first moved to North Carolina, Craig said he was sorry we came because there were no catfish in North Carolina. In Virginia, he caught a couple of 18 or 20 inch channel cats and was disappointed he had not any in our new state. So, I got some night crawlers and we went to Lake Wylie. Craig caught five channel cats between school letting out and dinner.

About the same time, Craig and I were fishing at Mountain Island Lake. Craig was mostly standing next to me, talking. He said, "Lots of families don't have a mommy." I agreed. Then he said, "Lots of families don't have a daddy." I agreed. Then he said, "And lots of families don't have a little boy so the daddy will have someone to go fishing with him." And I agreed with that too.

My current boat is a 17 foot Ranger R71. When Craig graduated from UNC Chapel Hill, the desire for a new boat began to gnaw at me. In the small bass club I belonged to, no one wanted to fish out of my boat. And it's true, the live wells in it were not sufficient to keep fish alive over a long day on the water. It was not as fast as other boats owned by club members. I contacted Cliff Shelby at Ranger Boats and Cliff helped me pick out a boat. I ordered it.

The boat was delivered to Hubert Greene in Spindale, North Carolina. Bill Shumaker rode over with me to pick it up. It was green and matched the color of my truck perfectly, though I had not anticipated that. Shortly after I got the Ranger, Craig and I were fishing at Lake Wylie. He asked what I did with the earlier boat. I told him I left it at Greene's on consignment and if someone would give me $1000 they could have it. Craig said he would give me that, so I went to Spindale and got the boat. When I got the Ranger, Craig was living in Wisconsin and I had not considered giving him the boat. Once he was back in North Carolina, doing so made sense.

Ranger has long touted their boats as unsinkable. Craig and I had an opportunity to test that. With the rest of the bass club, we were fishing Kerr Reservoir, Buggs Island to many, on the North Carolina-Virginia border. While some wandered out across the main channel, with Bill Shumaker and Harry Leamy in a companion boat, Craig and I decided the wind was too severe to leave Nutbush Creek. Indeed, a number of boats sank that day.

Slowly we made our way south on Nutbush Creek, an arm of Buggs Island as large as Lake Wylie. We were going into the wind and I was trying to ride up on oncoming waves deliberately, let the waves pass under the boat, then add a little power between the waves, and ride up the next one. Either I misjudged the speed or two waves came too close together, but water spilled over the bow and filled the boat ankle deep. Craig's tackle box floated and we were sitting in the lake, at least the portion of the lake in the boat. We were now heavy with little freeboard. The next wave did not spill over us, it washed over us. As it filled the boat, I thought, "Well, we're going to find out if Ranger boats sink." It did not, but it took 40 minutes for the bilge pump running full time to evacuate the water.

Currently at the cabin there are two boats, both aluminum. The 12 foot boat is a Sears and Dad bought it at least 60 years ago. We dragged that boat all over. One of our favorite spots was down the steep bank at Pickerel Lake. When Craig was a teenager, we wanted to fish Pickerel but Dad

Senior year in high school (I can tell by the baseball cap), I'm piloting the Sears boat.

said he would not go. The bank was too steep. Craig and I assured him we would handle the boat and help him up and down the bank. Once we got both Dad and the boat down the bank, Dad backed over something on the edge of the lake and fell into the water. Only his dignity was hurt. We each caught two pike in a five to seven pound range, and Craig did not catch his until we were almost ready to leave. He had been pretty disappointed until he redeemed himself.

The 16 foot boat at the cabin is a Starcraft. Dad often said about the boat, "They don't make boats like that anymore," implying the Starcraft was better than newer boats. Not so, Dad.

Long ago, Dad purchased Evinrude outboards to power the boats. One was a five horsepower and one a 9.9, the latter of course to avoid restrictions on engine size of 10 horsepower. Both engines were at least 45 years old. While neither had been abused, they had been used.

A few years ago, I took the Starcraft boat and 9.9 engine to Nawakwa Lake, not far from the cabin. Before I left the cabin, I pulled the starter cord and the engine fired. Once I got to Nawakwa and under way, the engine died and I could not get it started. I rowed back to the ramp and loaded the boat on the trailer. While I was fiddling with the engine, a chap appeared who claimed to be a small engine repair man from Jackson, Michigan. Just what I needed. He worked a few minutes, pulled the starter cord and the spring broke. Not something which could be repaired in the field. Back to the cabin. I put the six horse engine on the boat and it worked in the yard. Back to Nawawka and the second engine failed.

I loaded both engines in the truck and took them to the nearest Evinrude dealer in Curtis, roughly 50 miles away. A mechanic asked, "Where did you get those? I have not seen one like either of them for years." Mr. Watson, the owner, was not around, but the mechanic said he would look at the engines and see if one or both of them could be repaired. He told me to call tomorrow.

So, I called. The mechanic said the six horse was running but he would not guarantee it would ever run again. The 9.9 could not be repaired. As I pondered what to do, I wondered if the dealer would take either or both as a trade-in for a new engine. When I got to Curtis, I asked. Mr. Watson said he would give me $2000 toward a new Tohatsu 10 horse engine. Sold!

A little over a year later, on my next trip to the cabin, I took the Starcraft and Tohatsu to Nawakwa Lake. The engine fired and I made my way along a bank I had not fished before where I caught one small pike. When I came to a corner, another boat was coming my way, so I ceded that bank and headed across the lake. About 100 yards into the crossing, the engine died. And it would not start. The wind was blowing me across the lake, so I began to row hard to get back to the ramp lest I have to get back under my own power. The other boat approached and asked if I wanted a tow to the ramp. I accepted the offer.

After boat and engine sat in the cabin yard for an afternoon and night, I pulled the cord on the engine and it fired right away. So, back to Nawakwa Lake. In the sense of the engine's performance, it was a reprise. Engine started, ran a few minutes, died and would not restart.

Back to Curtis. I explained while the warranty had expired the engine only had 10 or 12 hours use. Turned out a plastic component of the carburetor was broken. When the engine got warmed up, the broken piece shut off the gas flow. Folks at the dealership said they were sure Tohatsu would honor the warranty (does that make me think lots of other folks had the same problem?) and the part would be ordered. Be fixed in 10 days. I was on my way out of the UP and told the dealer I would be back in two weeks and would come by and get the boat. When I called, the part was back ordered and would not be in Curtis for some time. The dealer suggested I take the boat to North Carolina and have a dealer there repair it. When I explained the boat and engine never left the UP, the dealer said to leave it with him for the duration I would not be in the UP. When I returned, he assured me, the engine would be ready to go. And the next year, it was. I have been reluctant, however, to take it where it might be hard to get back – like downstream on the Tahquamenon River.

In the fall of 1955, we bought a canoe. It was (and is) a 15 foot Grumman aluminum light weight model and weighs, I recall, 57 pounds. Though it has not been used for several years, it hangs in the garage, ready to go at a moment's notice. At one point, Dad ceded his share to Craig, but Craig now has his own canoe.

Among the early trips with the new canoe, we went down a portion of the St. Joseph River in southern Michigan. The St. Joe wanders from rural Calhoun County, through a corner of Indiana, back into Michigan and into Lake Michigan between St. Joseph and Benton Harbor. We put in at a bridge on a county road upstream from Clarendon and took out at 20 Mile Road downstream from the small crossroad. This portion of the St. Joe is upstream from what James L. Souers identifies as the headwaters in *A Paddling Guide for the St. Joseph River.* Mom provided the shuttle service, as she so often did.

Dad was eager to paddle the St. Joe because this portion was near the farm where he grew up. Several boys used the river as a fishing and swimming hole. Dad and Uncle Steve were often together in a small boat. I have a vintage photo of three boys in it. Dad claimed he and Uncle Steve shared ownership. Uncle Steve told me it was his boat but he let Dad use it.

Me in the stern, Dad in the bow, and Nancy seated as we canoe the St. Joe River.

We persuaded Nancy to go on the trip on the St. Joe with us. She was a reluctant companion for some reason. She said she would go, but would not help. At one point we had to drag the canoe over a log crossing the river and Nancy sat, imperial-like, in the vessel as Dad and I wrestled it over the obstruction. When Nancy read a draft of this chapter, she said, "At that point, my library book fell into the river, but it was retrieved. You were not happy that I brought a library book on such a trip."

It addition to its use at the cabin, Dad and I made several floats on the Manistee and AuSable Rivers. We caught some nice trout. When we fished the Manistee, we camped at a State Forest camp along the river. Based on Jim Bedford's *Flyfisher's Guide to Michigan* I presume the campground is now called Upper Manistee River Campground.

On one of the trips we had the misfortune of picking a day the University of Michigan dumped students and canoes in the Manistee. They came down in groups of five or six canoes, often tied together, careening from bank-to-bank, running into trout holding cover, and probably under the influence of too much wobblypop. At one point Dad and I were pulled off to the side of the stream, under some alders, to let a flotilla go by. A guide who had seen us on the water on other trips, also in a canoe, passed and saw us in the bushes. His client was dutifully casting. As he saw us, the guide said in a low voice, "Great day for dudes, isn't it."

On another trip on the Manistee, we came around a corner, fast. The canoe passed under a sweeper and I ducked. Dad didn't. The sweeper caught him under the chin and pinned his head to the panel over the stern. Each time he pushed himself free, the current drove his chin right back where it had been. On the same trip, at another corner we wedged the keel into a slot in a stump. We could not turn sideways to let the current carry us off the stump for fear we would swamp. We struggled backwards until we got off.

One day when we were on the Manistee, we decided to make a longer than usual float. We fished, floated, fished, floated some more. Mid-afternoon, Dad decided, since we did not know where we were and how long it would take us to get to the spot where we told Mom and Nancy to meet us, we should stop fishing and paddle. I was pushing hard enough I could feel the paddle bend with each stroke. We passed a cabin with several guys sitting in chairs along the bank. One of them said to me, "Young fella, the guy in the back isn't paddling."

I answered, "As long as he's not dragging the anchor."

Further downstream, still paddling rigorously, we swept around a corner where a man was standing in the river. We were moving fast, right at him. If we hit him, we would knock him into the water. As we shot past his shoulder I said, "Excuse me, sir, we're going right through your hole." He was startled but did not fall.

When we finally got to the takeout point, Mom and Nancy had been waiting several hours. They did not know where we were, when we might arrive, if something terrible had happened. As I look back, Mom put up with a lot of crap.

We never did as well on the AuSable. It is one of the world's famous trout streams. Grayling, Michigan, on the AuSable, is the founding site of

Trout Unlimited. On one of our trips Dad and I were alternating in the stern. Guy in the bow fished and the guy in the stern tried to maximize the fishing opportunities. My turn in the stern. I held the canoe close to the bank. Rather than paddle, as I wished to reposition the canoe, I let go of the alders I grasped to hold the canoe, let the canoe drift a few feet and grabbed a new branch. Suddenly, at least from Dad's perspective, the canoe shot into the current and ahead several feet. Dad turned and asked, "What are you doing?" I nearly grabbed a branch with a paper wasp nest and shook the nest into the canoe.

Many years later, when we lived in northern Virginia, the canoe got plenty of use. On Craig's first fishing trips, we took it to Goose Creek Reservoir and fished for panfish and catfish. I bought a push button reel and rod combo for Craig. Once when I was casting and giving Craig the rod to fish, he told me, "Daddy, you have to throw closer to that rock. That's where they are." When Craig caught the catfish, the ones which caused him to think we should not have moved to North Carolina, I kept my hand under his rod to prevent it from being jerked out of his hand. But he caught the fish himself. On the trip home, I said, "You thought you were going to have the rod pulled out of your hand, didn't you?" He agreed.

We also fished Goose Creek itself with Jere Richardson, Jr. I had an electric trolling motor and we went upstream from the bridge where we put in and got away from the anglers close to the road. One day it rained the entire time we were on the water. The boys fished through it, caught a bunch of bluegills and sunfish and had a wonderful time.

The last time we went to Goose Creek, Craig was already seated in the bow and Jere was standing near the stern. I had the battery and was about to lower it into the canoe. Jere volunteered to help. "It's heavy," I warned him. He assured me he could lower it safely, but it clunked onto the bottom of the canoe. As we made our way upstream, I noticed water around my feet, lots of water. I lifted the battery and exposed a hole in the canoe where the battery hit. We turned around, got help from the stream by anglers near the bridge. Jere, Sr. asked if he should pay to repair the canoe. I told him Jere and I shared responsibility for the damage. Jere should have said he was not certain he could hold the battery and I should have known better than think an 11 year old boy could hang onto a 70 pound weight. I patched the hole with a piece of airplane aluminum and some liquid steel.

While writing this chapter, I purchased a new boat – a kayak. I bought a Hobie Outback, the kayak I wanted rather than the kayak I could afford. This is a fishing kayak, propelled by fins operated by foot pedals as well as paddles. Its first trip was a seven mile float down the Uhwarrie River in North Carolina. I took it on a solo trip to Quetico Park (See Chapter 27, "Alone, but Not Lonely.")

Kenneth Grahame, in *Wind in the Willows*, has Water Rat explain to Mole, "Believe me, my young friend, there is <u>nothing</u>—absolutely nothing – half so much worth doing as simply messing about in boats." That's what I think, too.

Chapter 5
The Log

All the wise anglers, at least so I was told, kept a log. Where they fished, what worked and what didn't. Starting August 28, 1952 I began a comparable book. The last entry is July 17, 1964. Robert Traver in one of his classics, *Trout Madness* (1960), mined his log for material. So, I am in good company, even if Traver's notes carry more weight.

What did I learn? Reading the entries now, much of what I learned is not included. Even reading between the lines does not reveal many lessons. Here is a selection of log entries and what I think now, more than 50 years later.

August 30, 1952, Saturday. Shore out to middle, water choppy early, calm later. Pickerel Lake, 11:00 to 8:00. Lazy Ike and Shad River Runt. Got my limit: 5. From 14" to 19 ½. (Fast retrieve.)

What the log does not tell, Dad, Mom, Nancy and I went to Pickerel to fish for perch. I was much more interested in catching pike and I cast as often as I could between assisting in perch catching. A key lesson on this trip was how to vary the retrieve of a lure, like a River Runt, over pockets in the pond weeds. If I reeled slowly, the River Runt made its way over the nearly emergent weeds. When the lure came to an opening, a faster retrieve made the lure dive. That's where I caught my fish.

Many years later I was on the phone with Lisa McDowell Snuggs when Lisa worked at PRADCO, maker of the River Runt. When Lisa said PRADCO was discontinuing the River Runt, I insisted it was a great lure, one of my all-time favorites. She asked me how long it had been

Clare Piepkow, left, Bob Pierson in the center, and me on the right before Clare fell in the trout stream.

since I bought one. "Twenty years," I answered.

It was the first time I caught a limit of pike. Mom and Nancy got tired and we took them to the car. Dad took me back out to catch the last two, I presume because he knew I would like to brag about my success. Another time Mom and Nancy took the short stick.

May 4, 1953, Sunday. Fox River, trout hitting fair, 3 trout kept (7" long). Went with Clare and Bob.

Clare Piepkow and Bob Pierson, high school students in Dad's shop class, went to the cabin with us. Dad obtained several thousand red pine seedlings from the US Department of Agriculture. Clare and Bob helped us plant the small trees. Now mature, the pines are scattered across the property.

We fished downstream of the Reservoir, west of Carpenter Lake. In a beaver pond, we could see trout milling around. In order to catch them, we had to stay below the dam and lob worms over the dam and into the pond. Clare decided he could reach where the trout were if he walked out on a log which extended into the pond a dozen feet. The log was four or five inches below the surface. Clare took a couple of steps, despite my warning the log was slippery, and dunked himself in the pond with only his head above water. We walked back to the cabin, about a mile and a half. It was spring, but still chilly. Several years ago Dad and I had a chance to talk to Clare and he recalled the soaking.

April 25, 1954, Sunday. Spring Brook, suckers running. Hard to catch because they don't take well. Caught one 20". Water high and swift.

Lee Reeve, a longtime friend and best buddy and I drove in Lee's car to Spring Brook, perhaps a dozen miles from home. White suckers were thick. But we did not catch many. Dad ground suckers and made fish cakes. Dad ate about any kind of fish.

June 25, 1954, Friday. In the evening we hit Grand Marais Creek. They were hitting worms frantically and flies fair. A ratio of 3:1 for worms. Main problem was lifting trout over the far side of logs. They hit a brown pattern better than grizzly (caught the trout on home tied fly).

Grand Marais Creek was shallow. Logs left from timbering in the early 20th century crisscrossed the stream. Trout laying under the logs picked a drifting dry fly as it approached sunken wood. I had to be quick to get a hook set and lift the trout to the downstream side of the obstruction.

Chances are the brown flies I was using were Royal Coachmen and the grizzly flies were Adams. I tied both in abundance. I also tied bivisibles in both colors, a pattern which seems to have dropped off the list of anglers. Dave Hughes' magnum opus, *Trout Flies: The Tier's Reference* published in 1999, offers only a one sentence reference to bivisible flies. A bivisible is a dry fly, a fly designed to float on the surface, tied with two colors of hackle.

A dark hackle is wound Palmer style from the bend of the hook forward to near the eye. The last couple of rounds of hackle are a highly visible color, traditionally white, to make the fly easier to see. Palmer is British usage for caterpillar, thus a Palmer-tied fly has hackle the entire length of the hook.

Dad usually outfished me. He was never a fly fisherman. Bill Yunk (see Chapter 1, "A Kid Starts Fishing") tried to teach him, but it did not take. Dad was strong and never accommodated to rhythm rather than strength as the key to fly casting. Once as we left Grand Marais Creek Dad noted I had fun catching trout on flies and having fun was the important part.

July 9, 1954, Friday. Trout on Grand Marais Creek hit flies quite well, a brown pattern working best (brown bivisible). Nancy caught a trout on worms and Dad caught quite a few. My main trouble remains striking. I'm too quick when it's light and too slow in the dark.

More than 60 years later, the "main trouble" lingers on.

Weather observations are more important! With no date attached, these words are scratched across the top of the next page. As the earlier notations reveal, I did not pay much attention to weather conditions. Perhaps because I rarely fished in inclement weather. In the 1950s I did not have quality foul weather gear as I do now. And I have never made systematic notes about barometric pressure as many anglers have. At one point I bought a thermometer, which I still have, and notions about water temperature began to appear in the log in 1955. Over the decades, my most important weather observation is that stable weather is better for fishing than changing weather. Three days of lousy weather offers better fishing than a good day, followed by a lousy day, followed by a good day – and vice versa.

August 1, 1954, Sunday. When the sun shone, the pike were willing to hit, but when the clouds over Carpenter Lake scudded between the sun and the lake they wouldn't hit. Since this happened most of the time I got one on a Punkinseed and one on a spoon and pork frog.

The Heddon Punkinseed was shaped like any of the small sunfish species and came in a variety of colors. There were dozens of two inch bluegills in Carpenter Lake and the pike gobbled them. Jim Curtis, son of the folks Dad and I built the cabin for (see Chapter 2, "The Cabin"), introduced me to the Punkinseed and for several years it was my go-to on Carpenter Lake. A silver Silver Minnow with an Uncle Josh green pork frog was also productive and I still use that combination.

February 5, 1955, Sunday. Clark Lake. Lloyd Mercer, Dad and I. Perch hit cornborers on a Dipsey Darter better than fly. Gold better than silver. Perch 20' deep. Fourteen inches of ice.

Lloyd Mercer was the next door neighbor. We fished with him often. On this trip, we caught lots of fat yellow perch. Each of us had two holes in the ice, a couple of feet apart. In a circle with a 20 foot diameter we had six holes. We were at the northeast corner of the lake. At the southwest corner a blue Buick was on the ice; we recognized it as belonging to the town drunk. In a small village like Springport, such a lifestyle is readily apparent. About noon, the Buick left the ice, apparently taking the owner to lunch. In an hour or so, it came back and headed far across the lake. Then it turned and came right toward us. As it approached, a ripple in the ice nearly two feet high formed ahead of it. With six holes in the ice close together we debated whether to scatter or stay close in the event the Buick broke though and dumped us in the lake. We stayed. I still remember the sinking feeling as the ripple passed under my feet. The other angler ex-plained he merely wanted to know if we were catching any fish.

July 9, 1955, Saturday. Uncle Bill and I went to Bear Creek, but the caddis did not hatch enough to mention. Uncle Bill caught a nice brown and a small brook, leaving a fly in a big brown. I caught two brooks and a rainbow.

This is one of the few entries in my log including Uncle Bill. As I learned later, the insects were not caddis but mayflies.

April 28, 1956, Saturday. First day of trout season. Bear Creek high. Tried dry flies, wet flies, nymphs, bucktails. No luck. Snow, windy, cold.

Dad caught none on worms.

Uncle Bill and Ralph Hinckley also fished with us. I stuck it out long after I was chilled through; I did not want my colleagues to think I was a wimp. When I got back to the Club House, a small building Uncle Bill and some friends had near the stream, Dad and Uncle Bill were already there with a nice fire in the fireplace. Neither of them had any trout. Half an hour after I came in, Ralph showed up with a limit of trout, including a brown trout about 16 inches. Some folks really are better anglers.

July 30, 1956, Monday. Trout hit real well on North Branch of Stutts Creek, fair on the Middle Branch, on worms. Driggs River, brown trout on small Flatfish.

Clare Jones, Dick Jones, Orson Curtis, Dad and I made an excursion to several creeks south of Munising, Michigan. The streams were small and enclosed with alders. Poking a worm through branches, dropping it into the water, and snatching any trout out quickly was the only way to catch fish. By 10:00, I had a limit, 10 trout. The others had half a dozen among them. It was before the day of catch-and-release and we ate the fish. On the way home we stopped at the Driggs River.

I took no creel; I was going to release any fish I might catch. With my spinning rod, I rigged a small, orange Flatfish, attached a couple of tiny split shot to provide enough weight to cast and began fishing upstream from the bridge. I went perhaps 90 feet, cast toward a corner with a log. Bang. Big trout. I soon saw it was a brown trout and I had never caught a brown. Mr. Jones and Mr. Curtis were walking along the stream. I yelled to get their attention as I was sure I would not land the fish; they did not hear me. The trout got downstream of a log, dove under it, weakened and floated above the log and downstream. I was sure I would lose the fish now. I reached down, got the line and pulled the trout upstream of the log, let it drift below the log and then landed it. It was a 14 inch fish, at the time the biggest trout I ever caught. I have a cedar silhouette and cherish it yet, though I have since caught many larger brown trout.

From then on Dad and I often fished the small Flatfish with success for trout. One day on the Sturgeon River outside Wolverine, Michigan we both caught a nice mess of trout on small Flatfish. Lures with multi-colors did not work. When we came together one of us caught trout on a silver lure and one on a gold, but they had to be a solid shiny color.

June 28, 1958, Saturday. Manistee River, State Campground to M-72. Live caddis on stream brought trout to surface. Action was good on poppers and dry flies. Flatfish did poorly. Jim Weil teased one fish (12") into striking a rubber spider even though it dragged across the surface. He just kept casting to a rising fish. It seems trout can be teased into striking. The Adams was the best dry fly and white was the best popper.

Jim Weil was a high school buddy. He, Dad and I made a trip to the Manistee. Jim and I floated in the canoe and Dad ran the jitney. I wrote Ray Bergman, Fishing Editor of *Outdoor Life,* about Jim's success in teasing or provoking the trout to strike and got a nice response, one of several letters I exchanged with Bergman.

At this point, the entries fall off. After 1960, I rarely made it home during the summer. I was in graduate school and had a 12 month job at The George Washington University managing Adams Hall for Men. When I did get home, fishing was sporadic and I made desultory notes. For better or worse, I never renewed the effort with the log book. Would I be a better angler now if I had?

Dad's big pike.

Chapter 6
Dad's Big Fish

Despite the myths, all the big fish don't get away.

Dad's big pike was caught late August, 1975 on our first fly-in trip in Ontario. For many years Dad and I talked about going pike fishing in Ontario, hiring a guide, the works. Thanksgiving week in 1974, Mom listened to our talk and took me aside. "If you and Dad are going to make that trip, you better do it pretty soon," she said. With that admonition, I spoke to Nancy and she said we should do it. Dad made the arrangements with White River Air Service to fish Garnham Lake.

When we got to White River, folks at the air base wanted to take us in Friday evening rather than Saturday morning. The party at Garnham wanted to come out early and the outfitter would be saved a flight if we went in a day ahead of schedule. How about the guide? A chap told us not to worry about the guide, "Fish the bays and points," he said, "You'll catch all the fish you want."

During the first few days we caught lots of walleyes and pike, some casting and some trolling.

Tuesday evening our big fish story began. We were fishing behind a small island and into a bay of perhaps 10 acres, filled with pond weed. Dad was trolling with an orange with black dots S3 Flatfish, one he purchased at some department store for 95 cents and which he often used to remind me of his frugal ways. A huge pike swirled under Dad's lure, missed it, turned and smashed the lure. Dad's line broke on the impact.

Later Dad speculated his line may have been wrapped around the rod tip as a result of lifting and dropping it to steer his lure past weeds. Dad asked how big I thought the pike was. "Oh, about 10 or 12 pounds, I guess," I told him. In the cabin Dad switched from eight pound test to 15 pound test line.

Garnham is a large lake, eight or nine miles long, with many bays and coves and a couple of smaller lakes tacked on the north end. We were staying in a cabin at the south end of the lake and most of our fishing was done within a few miles of camp.

Part of our time was spent in the business of living – cooking, cutting wood for the stove, and other chores. One of the "other chores," in fact, was caused by cutting wood. Dad was chopping wood in the cabin and the jarring knocked the chimney down. I clambered onto the roof to make repairs and Dad tossed the axe to me. It slipped down the steel roof and into the lake. We could see it, 10 or 12 feet deep. With a long-handled rake tied to a stick to extend its length, we got the axe back. The axe plays a part in later tales.

Every day, we went back to the bay where Dad raised the big fish. We caught pike in the pond weeds and pike and walleyes around the deep edge of the leafy cover. None, however, were as large as the one missed and it lingered in our thoughts even when we were not talking about it.

Mid-afternoon on Thursday, August 28, well…here's how I recorded the event shortly after we got home.

"…Early [Dad's name was Earl and I often referred to him as Early] was trolling along the surface, very slowly, just enough to make the orange U20 Flatfish (he did not have another S3) wobble side-to-side. As we got to the spot where the fish broke off Tuesday, there was a great boil under Dad's lure. We both swallowed hard. It takes a big fish to make a splash like that.

"We kept on for about 30 yards before we stopped to reconnoiter. Dad said I should cast to the spot, which by now we both knew. Though I had some misgivings about trying to catch Early's fish, I thought our best chance was to show it as many different plugs as we had. With a long cast beyond the hole in the weeds, I brought my silver Rebel right over the hole where the big fish must be laying. Nothing.

"Dad kept on course and as his Flatfish with its crazy wobble/wobble/wobble neared the hole I could feel my excitement build. When it got right to the spot, all hell broke loose.

"The fish took it from just below the surface, dove and peeled off about 80 feet of line. Early was hanging over the stern with his rod pointed down toward the water. He slammed the engine into neutral as I hollered, 'Let him go, let him go.' Though the fish was tearing into dense weeds, I figured it would be no use to try to stop it. Dad said later trying to halt the run had not occurred to him; he was just hanging on.

"As line stopped whirring off the reel, I picked up one of the paddles and started after the fish. I stuck the tips of unused rods under the seat in the bow to keep them out of the way. Leaning ahead, I could see under Dad's arm as the fish leaped out of the water, making a U-shaped picture against the forest beyond. I knew from the run this was a big fish, but when I saw it was the first I realized how big.

"Not adept at paddling a 16 foot boat, stern first, with a canoe paddle, sometimes I took Dad over his line entangled in the weeds, sometimes to the left and sometimes to the right. Dad shut the engine off. Little by little, he was getting line out of the tangle of vegetation. Sometimes Dad had two or three clumps of weed dangling from his line so the line made a big V between his rod tip and the water. I was sure while we were getting untangled from the weeds the fish would break off. Dad said he could still feel the throb of the big fish on the line.

"About 40 feet from the spot of the first jump, the big fish came out of the water again. Who says pike never jump? The fish made a big circle, and as he rolled back and forth trying to roll over the line, we could see the Flatfish laying aside his massive head.

"Suddenly, the last few feet of line came free of weeds. It was the first time since the initial strike Dad's line ran directly from rod tip to fish. The fish was not thrashing about now. It was swimming powerfully along, a few feet from a row of dead cedar trees along the side of the island. If the pike headed into the limbs, goodbye fish. The fish looked to me in control of what was happening.

"The fish veered toward the boat. I put down the paddle and picked up the net. A few weeks earlier I told a neighbor and angling buddy, I would have no qualms about landing a 20 pound musky with my new net, but it sure looked plenty small now. I eased it into the water.

"Closer and closer it came. I kept saying to Dad, 'He's not ready, he's not ready.' And Dad kept saying to me, 'That's right, that's right.' Now the fish and I were about four feet apart and he was swimming toward an open net.

"As the fish came within reach, I decided the longer the fish was in the water, the better it was for him and the worse it was for us, so I slid the net under his belly and gave the biggest, hardest heave I could. Over the side of the boat, I twisted the net to wrap the fish in it. Though I did not know it, the fish broke through the net. Dad said later he could see the head sticking out one side and the tail the other.

"When the fish hit the bottom of the boat I was right behind, covering it with my body. Dad discarded his rod and he, too, covered the fish. We had a little chuckle as we criss-crossed the paddles over the fish and I sat on the paddles. The net was busted, the handle bent, but we had the fish in the boat. Its head stuck under the center seat and the tail disappeared under the stern seat.

"For the first time in about 20 minutes, we both got excited. As I looked up at Dad, there were tears on his cheeks. Made my trip, right there.

"Half way across the lake, the fish flopped, scattering tackle boxes and paddles. When we got to the cabin we learned the flop smashed the Flatfish. After we crawled in our sleeping bags, Dad yakked like a kid at summer camp. After going a long time with no reply, Dad said, 'I'll bet you'd go to sleep if I kept quiet.'"

When we got to White River, we weighed the fish at a Hudson's Bay Company store; it weighed 24 pounds on the grocery scale. We called Uncle Steve and urged him to find a taxidermist. Nancy and Craig were at Nancy's mom's and we were heading to Grand Haven. Dad had the 40 inch fish mounted. I still have it. I also have the smashed Flatfish, a model and color no longer available. But most of all, I have the memories of Dad's big fish and the time we had together.

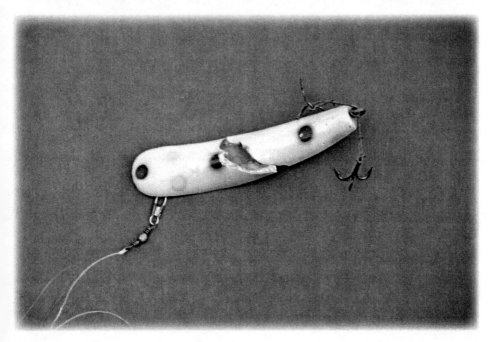

The broken Flatfish.

Chapter 7
Snowshoe Adventure

For my 68th birthday, I bought a pair of snowshoes from Cabela's. The folks near Dundee, Michigan had them on sale.

The Mead family has owned a cabin in the Upper Peninsula, about 12 miles from Lake Superior, since the early 1950's (see Chapter 2, "The Cabin.") We often went there deer hunting and for Thanksgiving. Those were trips in November and there was snow on the ground. We went late one April to plant pine trees and a time or two for the opening of trout season. Yet, I had never been to the cabin in dead of winter. I've had a long-time notion that I wanted to cruise through the woods on snowshoes.

Two birds with one stone or two things I wanted to do with one trip. With my new snowshoes, I headed for the cabin.

Some of the things I needed I anticipated. For example, I arranged with friends to leave my truck near the highway. I borrowed a folding shovel from Bill Shumaker to clear the snow from the door. (It occurred to me, while I was contemplating this trip, that I would need a shovel to clear the door. I knew there was a shovel in the work shed, not to worry. The work shed, however, is locked and the key is in the cabin.)

Mark Monsebroten, a friend from Manitoba, said I should have ski poles. I stopped in Dundee to purchase some. Cabela's was mobbed! Big sale going on. The chap who was in the area where ski poles were usually sold had none. In the bargain section of the store, however, I found a single ski pole with some of the cork on the handle damaged. The sticker price was $99.00, reduced from $179.00. Too much! I challenged the price to one of the sales staff. He said he would check it out and came back a little later with a price of $20.00. So I bought it. Good thing I did.

Some of what I needed, I had not anticipated. A sled, for example, to get gear back to the cabin. I packed all my gear in a large Duluth-style backpack. Fortunately, a friend loaned me a sled used by her grandchildren.

Making my way to the cabin

Earlier, I stopped in Newberry to get groceries. It was shortly after 1:00 when I got to the saw mill. I stashed the groceries in the backpack, loaded up the sled, including a gallon of water to prime the pump, and headed out.

For the first three quarters of a mile, I followed the groomed snowmobile trail easily without snowshoes. When I got to the trail to the cabin, however, I needed the snowshoes. Snow was about three feet or more on the level.

As the sled was quite narrow (about the width of a grandkid's fanny), the big backpack tipped off at least three times in the quarter mile back to the cabin. New to snowshoes, I had to turn around and re-load the sled. An article in *The New York Times* a while back claimed that learning to snowshoe was a 12-step program – once you have taken 12-steps, you've got it. Perhaps that is true over groomed trails, but it is not quite the case – at least for old goats like me – on deep, soft snow.

When I got to the cabin, snow was up to the window sills on all sides. Not drifted snow. Piled snow. With Bill's shovel, I cleared off enough snow to open the storm door and the top of the propane tank to turn on the gas.

In half an hour, I had the pilot lights on the stove and the space heater on. Water I left last summer to prime the pump was frozen and the gallon of water I brought was not quite enough. I began melting snow and the water I saved last summer. With a little more water, I had the pump operating as well.

It was after 4:00, so I settled in to read, get some dinner, and go to sleep.

Snowshoes stashed at the end of the groomed snow machine trail.

Expeditions

I had several day hikes in mind. Only one of them came to pass as I had planned.

When I got up the first morning, about five inches of new snow had fallen. Snow back in the woods is not like snow out by the road. After a few days, snow by the road takes on a gray cast. After a week or so, the snow adjacent to the road is dirty and lumpy from snow tossed up by plows.

Back in the woods the snow is white. Really white. And smooth. The first morning, there were no critter tracks. Later a snowshoe hare passed near the creek and even later another in front of the cabin.

About 10:00, I put on my polypropylene underwear, heavy jacket, fleece headcover and headed out. With my snowshoes, I headed down toward the lake to what was the first cabin at the lake. At each step, I dropped a foot or so into the snow before the combination of the area of the snow shoe and the packing of the snow would hold me. It would have been a fierce struggle without the snowshoes.

Once I got to the lake, I wandered over to Sam's cabin and south along the edge of the lake another quarter mile. Then I turned back and through the woods to another cabin. From there, I went back to my cabin. This short excursion took a couple of hours.

I took lots of pictures of the frozen lake, the cabins with snow on the roofs, the snow in the forest.

The next morning, I headed across Carpenter Creek back of the cabin. Piled snow nearly obscured the path of the creek. Carpenter Creek is only four or five feet across and shallow. To my dismay, I learned the snow over the creek was not solid enough to stand on. I dropped from the bank into the creek, with snow piled waist high ahead and behind. With the aid of my one ski pole and the alders along the creek, I dragged myself back onto the snow. Perhaps the most accurate descriptor would be to say that I "wallowed" in the snow bank until I clambered to the top.

I made my way downstream to the confluence of the two branches of Carpenter Creek. I took some pictures of the abandoned beaver meadow and made three more crossings of the creek. In the first, I made the same mistake I made before, with the same result. On the second, I also broke through the snow, but I learned the crampons on the bottom of the snowshoes were useful to help get out of such spots. I jammed the snow with the snowshoe until it was packed and then the crampon would hold and let me climb up. The last time I crossed the creek, I found a spot that looked secure and then took several short, quick steps and got across before the snow bank collapsed. Who says old dogs cannot learn new tricks!

Some of my favorite vistas have been along the west branch of Carpenter Creek. There was a massive white pine on the bluff above one of the abandoned beaver meadows. It stood in contrast to the bare deciduous trees.

From there, I headed up a bluff bank, over to an abandoned timber trail, and back to the groomed snow mobile trail. Then back to the cabin. This was the hike I had planned. It was all I had anticipated.

The next morning, I headed along the groomed trail toward the cabins on the southwest corner of the lake. I left the trail and hiked back toward several cabins, including one Dad and I built in the summer of 1954 and to the new cabin that replaced the A-frame down in the corner of the lake where I have caught so many pike.

I debated a hike to a large beaver pond or to a small lake in the back country, but decided to head back to the cabin. I was already a couple of hours into my hike and thought that was enough.

When I stopped in Newberry for supplies, I purchased enough for three days in the bush. Now I had to decide whether to go get more food or head home. I chose to head home. But I plan to do it again.

Thoughts

Over my lifetime, I have spent lots of time in the boreal forest. As a youth, I cruised the area around the cabin. As an adult, I have wandered that area and spent 20 years – off-and-on, mostly on – in Quetico Park in Ontario. But this was different.

It was so quiet. Simon and Garfunkel sang about the "sounds of silence." Once I heard what I thought was a woodpecker; Kenn Kaufman, *Lives of North American Birds*, indicates only the Hairy Woodpecker or the Downy Woodpecker might be in the north woods during winter. But there were no birds fluttering around, no squirrels or chipmunks chattering to one another – none of the white noise of the forest. While at the dining table in the cabin, I saw an unidentified raptor fly toward the lake.

The snow was so white, so pure. After a severe wind, which occurred one day, there were spots on the snow where the collection on trees had dropped. Otherwise, the snow was unmarked and brilliantly white.

Snowshoeing is strenuous work! Each day when I got back to the cabin, my clothes were soaked with perspiration. After the first hike, before I left the cabin I filled a large stew pot with water so I could heat water as I took off my clothes and bathe nearly immediately. It would have been jolly cold to allow the perspiration to evaporate. Snowshoeing is an aerobic activity. All the squats and lunges I have done at the gym sure paid off on this trip.

It was cold. As those who have lived in snow country will understand, the dry snow crunched at each step. Of course, such snow does not pack very well, and that's why at each step I sank into the snow pack a foot or so. Most mornings, it was 10 degrees F. One afternoon, after the snow had fallen of the roof, the sunny side of the cabin reached 28 degrees F. Inside the cabin, I was comfortable, though it was very warm near the ceiling and cold on the concrete floor. I'll need to have better slippers when I return.

And, yes, I plan to return.

Chapter 8
Wit and Wisdom of Izaak Walton

Izaak Walton wrote, among things, a small treatise on fishing titled *The Compleat Angler*. Walton's book, published in 1653, has never been out of print. It is filled with observations on life and angling. For those of us alive and angling, there is abundant wisdom and no small amount of wit in Walton's book. Outside my office door, I used to have a small sign indicating "International Headquarters Committee for the Beatification of Izaak Walton." No student asked who Izaak Walton was.

Walton's book is similar in one respect to what we have from Plato. It is in the form of a dialogue. Piscator is the protagonist, the authority who engages others in conversation. Piscator comes from *Pisces*, the Latin word for fish. And is true of the Platonic dialogues, sometimes Piscator's challenger raises the weakest argument, not the strongest, making Piscator's success foreordained. While others appear, Piscator's principal companion is Venator. They spend several days together, wandering about the countryside, staying in inns and meeting persons along the road. All the while Piscator explains to the willing Venator fishing and life.

The Compleat Angler is organized into a series of chapters. In the original version there were 13 chapters, but by the fifth edition of Walton's work it had ballooned to 31 chapters.

Walton addressed his book, "To all Readers of this discourse, but especially to the honest Angler." Which of us would admit to being a dishonest angler? Thus, Walton addresses us all.

At the core of Walton's approach is the notion that angling can be taught, but never mastered. As Walton first explains, "For Angling may be said to be so much like the Mathematicks, that it can never be fully lernt;

Line drawing of Walton, circa 1890, from a children's book.

at least not so fully, but that there will still be more new experiments left for the trial of other men that succeed us."

Consider, as examples, the "new experiments" anglers my age have experienced. The first time I tried plastic worms, they were as close to the color and shape of earth worms as possible. I rigged them as described on the package and tried to catch trout on a small stream in Michigan. The cold water stiffened the worms into rigid lumps and an oil slick rose to the surface above the worms. Now, soft plastics are a hallmark of fishing for virtually every species in salt and freshwater. They come in an array of shapes, colors and representations. Or consider, as a "new experiment." the use of electronic imaging while fishing. As a young angler, I found out how deep the lake was because I tied a red string through the anchor rope at one foot intervals. What the future may portend I don't know, but I suspect it will contain sufficient "new experiments" to challenge Walton's followers.

Walton, walking with Venator and Auceps, asserts he is "a brother of the Angle.... [possessed of] that simplicity which was usually found in the primitive Christians, who were, as most Anglers are, quiet men, and followers of peace." Many accept this model of fishing as simple contemplation, one with nature, kids on a creek bank only partly hoping they will catch a fish. Among the protagonists of this view is one of North America's best writers, John Gierach whose work appears regularly in *Fly Rod and Reel* and is collected in books with wry titles like *Death, Taxes and Leaky Waders; Sex, Death, and Fly Fishing;* and *Standing in a River Waving a Stick*. As is true of *The Compleat Angler*, Gierach's writings are only superficially about fishing.

Followers of tournament fishing, for bass or walleyes or whatever, know such angling is neither simple nor contemplative. Walton's model scarcely fits what often appears as the publically dominant pattern of fishing, while probably not the most common one.

Angling, Walton thought, was "an art, and an art worthy the knowledge and practice of a wise man....[and] he that hopes to be a good angler, must not only bring an inquiring, searching, observing wit, but he must bring a large measure of hope and patience, and a love and propensity to the art itself; but having once got and practised it, then doubt not that angling will prove to be so pleasant, that it will prove to be, like virtue, a reward to itself." For non-anglers, it is often difficult for them to fathom that going fishing is the reason to go fishing. It's not to catch fish, watch the sun come up or go down, see deer come to the water to drink or any of the myriad collateral benefits of a day on the water. All those are side benefits.

Walton believed angling worthwhile, in part, because it stood apart from many activities of men (a modern writer would be constrained to include women). He wrote, "…in ancient times a debate hath risen, and that it remains yet unresolved, whether the happiness of man in this world doth consist more in contemplation or action?" Walton's resolution was simple. Happiness, he wrote, was where "these meet together, and do most properly belong to the most honest, ingenious, quiet, and harmless art of angling….the very sitting by the river's side is not only the quietist and fittest place for contemplation, but will invite an angler to it."

Nonetheless, Walton's book contains plenty of "how-to" contemporary anglers will recognize. He hoped when one went fishing, "…that if he be an honest Angler, the east wind may never blow when he goes a-fishing," and if "…the sun is got so high, and shines so clear, that I will not undertake the catching of a Trout till evening…." or, "…if you fish for him on the top, with a beetle, or any fly, then be sure to let your line be very long, and to keep out of sight …"

One of Walton's observations was brought home to me a couple of years ago fishing rainbow trout on the Copper River in Alaska. Walton wrote, "…so, my scholar, you are to know, that as the ill pronunciation or ill accenting of words in a sermon spoils it, so the ill carriage of your line, or not fishing even to a foot in a right place, makes you lose your labour: and you are to know, that you may have my fiddle, that is, my very rod and tackling with which you see I catch fish, yet you have not my fiddle-stick, that is, you yet have not skill to know how to carry your hand and line, nor how to guide it to a right place: and this must be taught you; for you are to remember, I told you Angling is an art, either by practice or long observation, or both." Dr. Max Hillberry and Dann Crist were catching lots more and larger Copper River trout than I. Often I could see monster rainbows feeding only a few feet from where I was standing. Max and Dann were, simply put, better at mending line to get a natural drift in the feeding lanes where the trout were. Both made diligent efforts to teach me, and I did improve as a result of their efforts, but I lacked their "fiddle stick."

Among Walton's insights, and one I like most, came when he was instructing Venator in the ways of trout. Venator bemoaned the loss of trout, line and hook. Walton said, "Nay, the Trout is not lost; for pray take notice, no man can lose what he never had." Fishing for steelhead in northern Michigan, I reminded Squeak Smith of Walton's thought. A silver rocket grabbed my fly, headed downstream, jumped, and was gone. Squeak, before we started, told me I would lose more steelhead than I caught. I never had that fish, so I did not lose it.

Part of becoming a successful angler, according to Walton, are days when fishing is tough. He wrote, "Well, scholar, you must endure worse luck sometime, or you will never make a good angler."

Periodically, in their meandering, Piscator and Venator met milk-maids. Were these erotic encounters? It is never clear. Yet, the milk-maids were paid in fish for songs and entertainment.

Comparable to modern angling books, *The Compleat Angler* contained instructional chapters specific to fish an English angler in the 1500s would be likely to encounter.

Walton lived a simple life. He worked trading as an ironmonger in the early 1600s. A Royalist, Walton entered an early retirement after the defeat of his party in the mid-1640s. He purchased a farm near Shallowford which included river frontage.

He spent the remainder of his life visiting others who enjoyed fishing and gathering material for his classic. Walton knew some readers, "... may be liable to some exceptions, yet I cannot doubt but that most readers may receive so much pleasure or profit by it, as may make it worthy the time of their perusal, if they not be too grave or too busy men." In writing about fishing, Walton judged "to make a recreation of a recreation."

Among the songs and poems sprinkled about in *The Compleat Angler* is a poem attributed to W. B. titled, "The Angler's Song." The first stanza captures the essence:

As inward love breeds outward talk,
The hound some praise, and some the hawk,
Some, better pleas'd with private sport,
Use tennis, some a mistress court:
But these delights I neither wish,
Nor envy while I freely fish.

Wisdom there for Walton's age and ours. On those days Walton said, "I have laid aside business, and gone a-fishing."

Chapter 9
Misadventures

Any life filled with adventures must have a few misadventures. Menajobu was among the mythical characters of the Ojibawa. Not really an evil character, he just made mischief. For example, when a loon went after one of Manajobu's fish, Menajobu yanked the loon's legs so hard they were pulled to the rear of the bird's body. Even now, loon's legs are so far to the rear the birds have difficulty walking. According to legend, Menajobou invented the canoe. Yet, his influence, or those who paralleled his, have instructed my own travels.

Dad and the Rock

In the summer of 1954 (see Chapter 2, "The Cabin") Dad and I built a cabin across the lake from our cabin and added onto ours. We often had time to do some fishing. Late one afternoon we headed to the Sucker River to catch some trout. We usually headed in different directions, one upstream and one downstream, with an agreement about when we should rendezvous at the car. On this occasion, I went downstream and Dad up. The Sucker River is an easy stream to wade. I fished perhaps half a river mile, quite a way. Then it was time to leave the water and head back.

At that point in the Sucker's meandering to Lake Superior, the stream has cut through sand dunes and created a canyon 100 feet deep. Because I did not want to push my way through the dense alders along the bank, I climbed to the top of the sand dune and walked toward the car. As I did, I picked up a small stone – perhaps as large as a tennis ball – and heaved it toward the river. It soared and then fell harmlessly into the alders.

Wait a minute! I was a high school outfielder and I had a better arm than that. I put down my fly rod, picked up a stone more nearly the size of a softball and threw it hard and high. It came down in the river with a great and immensely satisfying splash.

Dad hollered, "Hey, what's going on?" He had reversed course and followed me downstream, but I did not know it. He was tucked under the alders to obscure his approach to any trout in the stream. I had not seen him. He said he did not see the stone come down, but suddenly the water at the end of his fly rod erupted.

Of course, it's funny now. But had the stone been a few feet to the left, it would have killed Dad, no doubt. And because I thought he had gone in a different direction, I would never have found him.

Stuck

Summer, 1964. It had been a couple of years since I had been to the cabin. I had just finished the Ph. D. exams, was no longer managing Adams Hall for Men at The George Washington University, and I wanted to go to the cabin. Mom and Dad both pled other obligations. Nancy, my sister, was reluctant to leave Springport as she was fretful her passport would not come in time for her to make a planned trip to Europe.

In 1964 the Michigan legislature redrew the lines of Congressional districts. Jackson County, where we lived, had been added to Congressman Chamberlain's district. Earlier in the year, I contacted Chamberlain, assured him I would campaign for him in the new county, and circulated nominating petitions for him. The Congressman and his staff knew who I was. I assured Nancy if she went to the cabin with me and her passport was not in the mail when we got back, I would call the Congressman and get it. So she went.

We loaded the canoe on my VW Beetle and headed north. It may have been the first time I crossed the Mackinac Bridge with the canoe atop the Beetle. Nancy recalled the trip along US 2 near Lake Michigan as "thrilling." She said, "As each 18-wheeler came at us, I was sure it was going to suck us in. Though you pulled as far to the right as possible, several times it looked like we might not make it." It was windy and the VW-canoe combination offered a large, light profile.

Nancy did not want to fish all day, every day. Part of what we did was explore. We found a lake one day, my log indicates it was Newton Lake, and went back with canoe the next day to fish. A moose swam across the lake. Only moose I ever saw in the UP. Once Nancy was hunched over in the front of the canoe as I fished. I asked if she was OK. She was reading.

On one of our exploring days, we were on a logging trail, west of the Old Seney Road. Where, I haven't a clue. Didn't then. It had rained hard a few days earlier and there were puddles on the trail. Each time we came to a puddle, I stopped and probed the bottom to see if it was solid enough to drive through. I'd seen Dad do this.

Satisfied this particular puddle did not pose a threat, I drove ahead. What I had not considered, however, the grassy hump in the middle of the two-track was higher than the clearance for the VW. I drove into the middle of the obstruction and hung up. Wheels were no longer hitting the ground.

We were stuck. Really stuck. Fifteen feet or so of water in front of us and a comparable amount in back. I tried to ditch water away from the puddle, but that really did no good as the undercarriage still rested on the hump in the middle of the trail. So, shift into forward, shift into reverse, try to rock the car until it got footing. Dig dirt from beside the trail to fill enough to get traction. Push and pull.

The rub with all this was, Nancy could drive a stick shift but she was not skilled enough to transition from forward to backward, or vice versa, to rock the car. Upshot: I drove and Nancy, she might have weighed 100 pounds, had to do the pushing. From front and back. All the loose dirt I shoved into the puddles merely ended up covering her as the wheels spun furiously through the mud.

So, I let my little sister, and she was really little, push me out of a mud puddle that I willingly drove into. The good news? She's still my little sister and loves me yet.

A Shock

Bill Shumaker and I were fishing Yoke Lake. Yoke is a portage lake a quarter mile north of the late Happy Landing Lodge, about 30 miles north of Emo, Ontario where we were staying. As we usually did at Yoke, we were steadily catching smallmouth bass and having a dandy time. Yoke Lake is shaped like a Y, each arm several miles long. Bill and I were on the western arm, a couple of miles from the landing.

Mid-afternoon it began to rain. Then hail. Hailstones half an inch to an inch and a half fell. When they hit, they hurt. Bill and I sought cover on a narrow point. We tied the boat to a tree and huddled under the canopy of white cedars. We still got hit with hailstones, but not so frequently as when we were on the open water. We both had top-quality rainsuits and we were not getting wet, but the driving rain made life outdoors miserable.

After half an hour, the hail let up, but the rain continued. We discussed our options and decided to make a run for the landing. Our boat was typical of those used by lodges in northern Ontario. It was a 16 foot runabout with a 20 horse, tiller steer, outboard engine. I was in the stern, running the boat.

The landing was a wooden ramp with space for four boats like ours. The ramp was angled into the water. Each boat was to slide up on the ramp. When Bill and I got to there, three boats were already in place. Our buddies left the water before we did. I slid the boat onto the boards. Bill jumped out and secured the line to the far side of the ramp. He began to unload gear from the boat and carry it to the shore.

I stepped out of the boat, onto the landing. Since I was in the stern, once out of the boat, I was standing in four or five inches of water. Not really a problem. It went with the territory and I had the shoes to accommodate it. While I was pulling gear from the boat, suddenly my lower legs tingled and shuddered. Lightning hit the lake somewhere. The shock travelled through the water and came to me. I did not see the lightning strike, but I felt it.

I ran to shore and told Bill, "The gear can stay in the boat. It's already wet and I'm not going to get electrocuted just to carry a rod and a tackle box up the hill." Bill stuck it out, but I quit.

How far away the lightning strike was, I have no idea. If it diminished in energy as it sped across the lake, I have no idea. Whether I was really in danger, I have no idea. But it was shocking!

The Windblown Canoe

Bill Toole went to Quetico Park with me in 2006. I told Bill if we made the one mile portage into Blackstone Lake we would have the lake to ourselves. Lots of feisty smallmouth bass, I assured him, and there's a great campsite on an island in the middle of the lake. In we go.

The portage was long, but it was not up hill and down dale. It took a while, but doable. We set up camp on the island. Shortly after, Bill was standing near a bluff bank when another camper started up the bank and said, "Oh, you're already here." So much for we'd have the lake to ourselves. Before we left, five campsites on the lake were occupied.

While I busied myself with something, Bill wandered around the island. In a few minutes, he came back and said, "There's another campsite at the other end of the island. Come take a look." I looked at the canoe. It was pulled up away from the water, perhaps 50 feet from the lake. Though it was not tied to anything, it was leaning against a bank of white cedar trees. I was satisfied the canoe was safe. So, I went to look at the other site.

When I got back to our site, first thing I saw was what I didn't see. Our canoe. I looked to the east, and there our canoe was, drifting across the lake. Bad words crossed my mind, but they did not bring the canoe back. (That's always true of bad words. Why do we bother?)

I figured, I would wait until the canoe came to rest somewhere. Then wade across the shallow spot between the island and the lake shore, and circle the lake until I could recover the canoe. It would be a difficult trek, but the canoe was already several hundred feet away and getting farther away by every wind gust. Bummer.

Bill, starting to strip, said, "I'll swim and get it." He rejected my reservations and started toward the lake.

"Well, if you're going to do that, take a paddle." How he was going to get the canoe back, he had not considered. Paddle in hand, into the lake he strode and began to swim.

I thought, he's going to be cold when he gets back. I gathered every bit of dry wood I could find and laid it in the fire pit. I was ready.

The canoe came to rest on the far bank, perhaps half a mile away. Bill made steady progress toward it, but it was still a "fur piece."

When I could see Bill was paddling toward camp, I lit the fire. By the time he landed, I had a rip-roaring fire.

Lesson learned: I never leave camp without the canoe tied to a tree. When I did my solo trip to Quetico Park with my kayak (see Chapter 28, "Alone, But Not Lonely"), I dragged it onto dry land and tied it to a tree or a couple of trees. Before Bill and I went to look at the other campsite, I considered the safety of the canoe and took too casually the prospect it would blow away.

Best part, Bill is still my friend.

It's a Flat. No, it's Two Flats

Summer, 2016. The Outdoor Writers Association of America was meeting in Billings, Montana and I was going to the conference. But before the conference, I planned to hit some of my favorite Montana trout streams. That included Rock Creek near Missoula.

Bill Shumaker and I often camped at US Forest Service Siria campground. I headed there. Siria campground is 26 miles from the Interstate and most of that is a dirt road, filled with pot holes, ruts, and rocks. Travel 20 miles per hour is too fast.

After a couple of days fishing, some good and some not so, I decided to drive out for dinner to the truck stop between Clinton and Missoula. All well enough.

On the way back, at roughly mile 20, I hit something. The dashboard flashed, "right front tire, 8 psi, 0 psi." Shucks, a flat on the right front. Bad news. The good news is, I have a hydraulic jack and a spare tire. Soft sand on a dirt road might not be the best place to change a tire, but it can be done. And, at 8:00, still light. Strong words aside, a doable thing.

I got out of the truck to assess the damage. It's worse. Both right side tires were flat. Whatever I hit took out two tires, not one. I moved the truck as far to the right of the single track road as possible to let other vehicles pass. Then I started to hike toward my camp, two miles away.

About a mile into my trek, all the time pondering how in the blue blazes (strong words again) I was going to recover from this, I came to two

Two flat tires at the same time along a Forest Service road near Rock Creek, Montana.

anglers in the river. I stopped and yelled, "I hate to bother you guys, but I'm in a bit of trouble."

From the far side of Rock Creek, one of them started wading toward me, "What's the problem?"

I explained. He grabbed the car keys to their vehicle and said he would take me to camp. On the way, he told me he and his sidekick were planning to camp along the Creek, fish in the morning, then head to Missoula. They would change their plans and camp at Siria campground and take me to Missoula tomorrow.

A couple of hours after leaving me at my campsite, I heard a yell inviting me to their camp. I responded I was already in my sleeping bag, and no thanks. Of course, all my grub was in the truck a couple of miles away. In the morning, my new friends called me over for coffee and breakfast. Who says there are not nice people in the world?

They took me to my truck and left me for a while, as I asked. As they fished, I changed my clothes, took my pills, did whatever.

They needed to be in Missoula at 10:00. We drove into town, another 40 miles from the intersection with the Forest Service road, and they left me at Les Schwab, a major tire store with several outlets. The manager at the store said his crew was already out, but he would call one of the other franchises. Turns out, in Montana, flat tires in the backcountry are common. They had a truck with an air compressor. If I knew the tire size, and I did, a truck would be by shortly to pick me up and recover me. Sure enough, in half an hour a young man came striding through the door. I stood up and said, "I'll bet you are looking for me."

Understand, this was 40 miles by Interstate, and 20 more miles by dirt road. And two new tires. It cost me nearly $1000 to be made whole. Yet, it was a positive misadventure. Good guys were willing to adjust their plans to rescue me. Les Schwab had the knowledge and equipment to get me back on the road.

Menajabou

Well, bad things happen. Considering the difficulty loons have walking on land, maybe he did not treat me badly after all.

Jack Murphy with the big carp he caught on one of his trips with me.

Chapter 10
Coached, Not Guided

Periodically I am asked why I am not a fishing guide, take people fishing and make lots of money. Friends suggest, I'm going fishing, why not pick up a few coins on the way. No way. For one thing, most guides do not make lots of money. More significantly, however, I don't want to put up with the mess guides handle daily.

I do, however, permit groups to auction off what I call, "coached, not guided" trips. A number of years ago Keith Sutton, then CEO of the Future Fishing Foundation, asked me to allow FFF to auction a trip and I agreed on a trout fishing trip in the North Carolina mountains or a pike fishing trip in Michigan's Upper Peninsula. In due course, I got a phone call advising me someone had purchased the trip and would be in touch. I never heard another word.

Yet, I do make good. Several years in a row Carolinas Medical Center – Mercy auctioned "coached, not guided" trips. Nancy, my wife, was Director of Volunteer Services there and as part of the United Fund drive I made trips available. One of them sticks in memory. A hospital employee purchased a trip for a favorite uncle. We made an effort to fish High Rock Lake, an impoundment about 50 miles from Charlotte and host to three Bassmaster Classics.® I waited in the parking lot for a few minutes before he came. It was pouring with recurrent lightning strikes. When the uncle arrived, unfortunately I cannot remember his name, I told him we could reschedule or wait until the storm passed, but I was not going while lightning was flashing. We rescheduled.

A few weeks later, we met in front of my house and went to Cane Creek Reservoir in Union County. Cane Creek is managed for trophy largemouth bass fishing. The minimum size is 18 inches. A week earlier I fished Cane Creek with Jimmy Campbell. Jimmy and I had done well and I thought the uncle and I could catch some fish on white spinnerbaits. On the ride to Cane Creek the uncle explained he fished the previous summer quite a bit. He said, "I think I went eight times last year." I did not say I went eight times some weeks. While we did not catch any trophies, the uncle caught three largemouth, all about 16 inches long, roughly three pounds. I was disappointed. He was delighted. Each fish he caught was greeted with whoops and hollers and claims this fish was the biggest ever. On the way home and somewhat more restrained, the uncle was sure these were the biggest bass of his angling career.

Lucille Howard asked me to auction a trip for the League of Women Voters. In turn, it was purchased by a member who wanted it for her sons-in-law, all three. If we were to fish for bass, I explained, my boat could not accommodate four persons. She said she would designate two of the three and I agreed to take the third on a subsequent trip. In turn, one of the sons-in-law and I began negotiating possible dates. Rain cancelled a couple. A business trip cancelled another. We finally reached agreement to meet at Wilson Creek in the North Carolina mountains for some trout fishing.

At the last minute, one of the brothers-in-law could not make the trip, so the one who had been in touch with me commandeered a friend. We made our way to the bridge across the stream near the abandoned town of Mortimer. In the early part of the Twentieth Century, Mortimer was a bustling town of 100 buildings with folks who worked in the timber industry and the railroad which paralleled the stream. A flood in 1916 wiped out the lumber work. Another flood in 1940 ended the town.

A hundred yards or so upstream of the bridge is a pool where I have caught trout in the past and we headed there. I rigged each of my guests with nymphs, tiny sinkers and strike indicators. Gordy Honey, a guide working the Kamloops area of British Columbia asked if I knew the difference between a strike indicator and a bobber – he said the difference was $2.95 at Walmart.

In the run just below the pool, each of them missed a couple of strikes. I showed them how to mend line to get as natural a drift as possible as we made our way upstream. Several times I told one of them, "There's a fish, right over there. Cast so your fly will drift right through the spot." I could tell neither of them believed I could see trout in water running over cobble rocks. To tell the truth, when Jon Madsen on Montana's Bighorn River told me he could see trout, I doubted him. (See Chapter 24, "Seeing is Believing.") Jon taught me well.

When we reached the pool, I could see several trout actively feeding. One angler was on one side of the stream and one on the other. After each drifted a fly through key spots several times, I dug in my fly box and got a #20 Ray Charles, a fly Jon Madsen used to good effect. I told the friend to give me his fly and I clipped it off and tied on the Ray Charles. The friend asked incredulously, "You expect me to catch a trout on that?" I said I did.

He roll cast the newly rigged fly upstream and the strike indicator drifted toward us. Within a few feet, the indicator dipped under water, the friend lifted his rod tip and the battle was on. He caught a 14 inch brook trout, much larger, he said, than any he had ever caught before. It was the beginning of their belief.

After stopping for lunch, we headed back upstream. The pool was occupied by other anglers, so we walked farther into places I had never fished. In a long run, there were numerous trout feeding. I could see them. With repeated, "There's one, right there," my colleagues began to see them as well. They could not pick one out on their own, but if I told them right where to look and what to look for, they could tell where a fish was. By the end of the day, each had caught about 10 trout. Squeak Smith, a good fishing buddy and one of Trout Unlimited's "Ten Who Made a Difference" in the fifty year history of Trout Unlimited, told me later he caught 20 on that day trout fishing Wilson Creek. I think my guests would have caught 20 as well had they had a better hookup to strike ratio. All-in-all, we had a good day and I drew lots of satisfaction in the enhanced skills of those with me.

Gene Vaughn worked for many years as a fisheries biologist for Duke Power, now Duke Energy. Applying his professional skills to community service, Gene helped a YMCA Camp, Camp Harrison at Herring Ridge, develop a small lake as a fishery. The lake is used for swimming and fishing by campers.

It also serves as a money maker for the camp. With Gene at the lead, the camp has a fishing tournament every spring. Anglers pay $1000.00 each for a morning of fishing with someone with a boat. Gene insists on calling the non-fishing boaters "guides," though when guys get in my boat I assure them I am not a guide but a coach. Unfortunately, I have missed the last couple of years, but I hope to return to Gene's guide roster next year. (In 2016, I returned to Herring Ridge and the tournament.)

Doubtless the most satisfactory of those trips for me was a year in which the two guys I took out were not anglers at all. They brought spinning rods with broken guides, reels with line so old they had no idea how long it had been on the spool, and no lures. As we sat in the boat waiting for the signal from Gene to start, one of them asked, "How long have you been fishing?" When I replied, "Seventy years," he told his buddy, "We better listen to this guy. He's been at this a while."

After half an hour or so, I could tell with the gear they had, they were not going to catch many fish though they both made efforts to do what I suggested. So, I dug in my rod box, got out two spinning rigs and set them up with unweighted plastic worms. I told them to cast the worms toward the bank and reel them back slowly. "If something jerks on it, you jerk back." They began to catch bass, one right after another. Gene's tournament is scored on one "biggest fish" per angler. As they caught additional fish, I held up the fish in the live well and the new entry and asked, "Which one do you want to weigh in?" One of them said I had more experience in judging fish than they and they trusted me to make the judgment. So I did. During the morning they each caught 15 or so and they had a wonderful time.

While I cannot remember their names, Paul was their boss and he had paid their entry fees. Paul, as they explained to me, was a serious outdoorsman. He hiked through the mountains, fished widely, and he really wanted to win the tournament. Periodically, as they caught largemouth after largemouth, one of them would ponder, "Wonder how Paul is doing?"

At the end of the tournament, all the boats were tied to a long pier and anglers were taking their fish for Gene to weigh. My guys were making no effort to bring their fish to the scale, but I saw Paul's fish weighed and I knew each of my anglers had a fish bigger than Paul's. I urged them to hustle and weigh in, "You'll be pleased, I know," and they were. They both respected and liked Paul, personally and as their employer, but they were delighted to beat him.

Another year I took two professional football players, one whose name I do not remember. The other was Tim Biabatuka. Tim played at the University of Michigan and for six years was the featured running back for the Carolina Panthers. Both, of course, were much bigger dudes than I. Gene considers both the largest fish weighed in and the smallest. One of the bass Tim caught was pretty small and before Tim tossed it back in the lake I said we should keep it as there would likely not be one smaller. When Tim's fish was weighed, it was, if recollection serves me, seven ounces. Another angler, however, had one so small it did not pull the hook on Gene's scale enough to register. At the awards ceremony I argued Tim should get the prize for the smallest fish as, "Nothing in God's creation weighs nothing." Acting as tournament organizer, master-of-ceremonies, and tournament appeals committee, Gene ruled against my objection.

Doubtless, for me the least satisfying experience coaching anglers was also at the Camp Harrison tournament. I drew two chaps who had not known one another previously, but were in parallel business positions. They spent the morning discussing the merits of in-house services compared to contracting out, different personnel evaluation systems, and other matters of business importance. By 10:00 I merely moved the boat along the bank, periodically suggesting a cast here or a cast there. I was not going to make the fishing important to them, so I let them do what was important.

Among the liabilities of being a fan of women's basketball at The University of North Carolina at Charlotte, is sitting near Judy Rose, the Director of Athletics. Judy and I have known one another for almost as long as I have been associated with the University. We served on a number of committees together. Somehow Judy learned that I permitted groups to auction off fishing trips. During a game, Judy asked if the UNC Charlotte Athletic Foundation could auction off a trip. I said, "Sure, why not."

The first year I did a coached trip for Judy I took an engineer and his teen-age nephew. We fished Mountain Island Lake, a Duke Energy impoundment near Charlotte. It was fall and largemouth and spotted bass were in shallow water. I rigged each with a shaky head jig and narrow plastic worm. We were soon jabbing at one another as though we had known one another for years. During the morning hours, both anglers caught fish. They whooped and hollered at one another and at me and I back at them. Neither could cast with precision, so when I said, "Right at the base of that tree," or, "Go right to the center of the fork in that log," the prospects they would be successful were indeterminate. Twice the nephew successfully cast precisely to the spot I suggested and each time he caught one. As we left, I asked him how many he thought he would have caught had he hit all the targets I suggested. As we separated, the uncle asked, "Are you going to auction off another trip next year? If you do, I'll bid on it."

Whether he made good on his determination, I do not know. Someone else, however, won the trip. While I was in Montana trout fishing, a woman called to tell me she purchased the trip from the Athletic Foundation and was giving it to a relative. She said, "They want to fish Stutts Creek at Lake Norman." I told her Lake Norman, a huge power impoundment north of Charlotte, was a possibility, but I had not fished Stutts Creek in 25 years and was not sufficiently familiar with it to be sure of any success. We agreed the relative, Jimmy, would be in touch with me.

In due course, he was. We agreed, over time, on several days when we would fish at Lake Norman. Those dates got cancelled, one after another. As fall passed into winter, we agreed to fish Wilson Creek. Those appointments, too, got sidetracked. When spring came, I proposed Mountain Island Lake, an impoundment just below Lake Norman. Jimmy, Nick, Jimmy's nephew, and I finally made it.

Though both had substantial fishing experience, most of it was in salt water with very different gear. By text message, Jimmy asked if I could furnish equipment and I said I could. I rigged two spinning rigs with single hooks. We would fish unweighted plastic worms. When we got to Mountain Island Lake, we went upstream almost to the Lake Norman dam. Jimmy was amazed that such a place existed so close to Charlotte and he did not even know it was there.

Almost immediately, each had a strike and missed it. At the lower end of a small island, Nick caught a nice spotted bass, perhaps a couple of pounds. We moved across the river and fished along the bank. Duke Energy was moving water through the lake and the current pin-pointed the location of fish. At one point, as I was positioning the boat, out of the corner of my eye I saw a swirl right where Nick's worm was. He said nothing, so I said, "Hah, you didn't think I saw that, but I did." All-in-all, a good day with pleasant guys.

Jack Murphy is the son of Wendy Shepard Murphy. Wendy was a student in one of my undergraduate classes and for a complex set of factors, she became and remains a dear friend. Though neither Wendy nor Pat, Jack's father, are anglers, Jack developed an interest in going fishing. When Jack was six or seven, Wendy asked if I would take Jack fishing. I agreed. It is now an annual event and if Jack lived closer, we would go more often.

Jack's experience started, as so many of us have, with worms and a bobber. To maintain a child's interest, something needs to happen. A can of worms, a hook and a bobber is a sure fire way to catch something. And we did. On the third or fourth trip, Jack was fishing and I was getting a second rod rigged with a fresh worm so Jack never had to quit fishing. When he caught one, I cast the worm into a likely spot, gave him that rod and took the one with the fish he caught and started the cycle over. I saw two carp swimming along the edge of a dropoff. I cast ahead of them and gave Jack the rod. The lead carp spooked, but the second moved down and toward the sinking worm. The bobber dipped and Jack lifted the rod. Game on!

I was concerned the carp would drag Jack and gear into the water, so I held lightly onto the rod and coached Jack. As big fish do, the carp moved slowly one way, then the other, until it was convinced something was wrong. Then the real fight began. In a couple of minutes, Jack got the fish close enough to the boat for me to scoop it into the net. We took some pictures to show Wendy and put the fish back in the water. As it turned out, Wendy wanted to see the fish in the flesh.

Jack Horan, a friend, is an outdoor writer for *The Charlotte Observer*. I sent Jack a copy of Jack Murphy's carp, a fish I estimated weighed 11 pounds, with a request the image run in the *Observer*. The next Thursday, it did. Jack Murphy, living in Memphis at the time, got a phone call from an excited friend, "Your picture is in the paper."

Jack, on his trips with me, has graduated to fishing for bass. He does pretty well. We have had to miss a couple of summers, but among the satisfactions of life has been the developing personality and angling skills of my young friend. Someday, no doubt, Jack will pass on the fishing heritage.

Half a dozen or more guides have told me, "I get a lot of satisfaction seeing someone catch fish. Watch them develop a skill I tried to teach them. Have a good time." Though I do not want to become a guide, being a coach confirmed for me the guides' perspective.

Chapter 11
Fascination with Pike:
One Angler's Lifetime Passion

It all started the summer of 1950. It was the year the Detroit Tigers faded the last week of the season and lost the American League title to the New York Yankees. In mid-summer, when my parents took my sister and me to Michigan's Upper Peninsula, the Tigers were safely in the lead. On that trip a life-long fascination with baseball was joined by another – pike fishing. We stayed in a cabin on the shore of Carpenter Lake. There were pike and perch in the lake. While dragging a red and white Bass Oreno around the lake, I caught a 14 inch pike. It was the biggest fish I had ever caught. It met the Michigan minimum size for pike and we ate it. I was thrilled. It's a thrill that has never faded.

My folks bought 90 acres near Carpenter Lake and built a cabin back in the woods (see Chapter 2, "The Cabin). My sister and I still own the property and use the cabin often.

By summer 1953 I was a diehard pike angler. I went down to Carpenter Lake every day we were at the cabin and fished all day. Mother let me keep the pork rind on my Johnson Spoon in a glass of water on the table so it would not dry out. One summer Uncle Steve flew to the Upper Peninsula to visit and he brought a fellow school teacher, Bill Bradford, with him. Mr. Bradford had just returned from Ontario where he caught monster pike and was willing, perhaps eager, to fill the head of a boy with tales of pike lots bigger than those I caught in Carpenter Lake.

Nonetheless, Mr. Bradford asked if I would take him down to the lake and help him catch some pike. Earlier in the day I fished hours with only a couple of fish to show for my effort. Along a hundred yards of shoreline,

Mr. Bradford raised a dozen or so and caught as many in half an hour, casting a red and white Daredevle, as I caught all day. All he did, and looking back I'm sure he knew, was fan the flames of my "thing" for pike fishing.

Outdoor writers of the time, and I read them voraciously, offered only minimal interest in pike fishing. Ray Bergman, then Fishing Editor of *Outdoor Life*, wrote in an article later reprinted in *Fishing with Ray Bergman* to the effect that pike fishing was a fine way to rescue a fishing expedition when more worthy quarry like trout were not cooperating. Ted Trueblood, one of my genuine heroes, claimed in *The Angler's Handbook* pike had two qualities attractive to anglers: they struck savagely and were willing to hit artificial lures, but that was about it. Others put down pike as "snakes" or "hammerhandles." Here were authors on whose every word I hung and they minimized the appeal of northern pike. I didn't get it. And still don't.

Sister Nancy and I display a stringer of pike, early 1960s.

Legends of monster pike swirled through my head. Izaak Walton in *The Compleat Angler*, first published in 1653, wrote of pike so large they tried to drag mules into the water. While I doubted any pike in Carpenter Lake was large enough to pull a mule into the lake, I knew deep in my teenage gut I was sure to catch a trophy there. Between visits to the family cabin and through the long winter, such visions danced through my dreams.

Both Bergman and Trueblood (and others) mentioned fly fishing for pike, but as a young man that was not practical for me. My first fly rod was an eight and a half foot bamboo rod Dad purchased at a warehouse auction for five dollars. It came with an automatic reel. Trueblood said a bass weight rod could handle pike, but this was no bass rod.

When son Craig was a teenager, we began to talk about catching pike on fly rods. On a fly-in to an outpost in Ontario we took our 4-weight fly rods. We were a little under prepared, but what the heck. We caught a few pike about four or five pounds. The highlight of the fly fishing trip was a 10 or 12 pound pike that grabbed Craig's popper and took off for parts unknown.

We started planning for more fly rod pike fishing. We were taking annual trips to Ontario's Quetico Provincial Park, a wilderness adjacent to the Boundary Waters Canoe Area in Minnesota (see Chapter 19, "Fly Fishing for Bass and Pike," in *Quetico Adventures*). One evening after setting up camp on a long point in LeMay Lake, Craig and I took the canoe and our fly rods to a small bay. Smallmouth bass and pike between five and 10 pounds were thick. After I lost my third or fourth deer hair bug, Craig admonished me, "Dad, you better switch to a wire leader. We did not bring enough gear for you to lose a bug every other fish."

A decade ago I made a trip to Phelps Lake in northeast Saskatchewan in search of trophy pike. I did not take any fly fishing gear. Mark Montesbroten, my guide, however, had a fly rod. He claimed he knew where a monster pike was hiding and assured me I could catch her with his rod. Though I did not raise the fish, Mark said about my fly casting, "You've done this before." In the week I was at Phelps, I caught a number of pretty

As I've been able to wander farther afield, I've had access to bigger pike.

good pike on Mark's rod, but none of the 40 inch plus pike I caught on conventional gear.

In the years since, both Craig and I have devoted significant energy to catching pike on our fly rods. We have better gear, now. We use 8 or 9 weight rods. These rods can handle a pretty big fish. At Phelps Lake and several lakes in Ontario, Craig and a couple of other angling friends and I have successfully targeted pike with fly rods, big pike (see Chapter 18, "Armed With Eight Weights and Zonker Strips, Tim and Craig Take on the 'Frog Thieves'").

Lots of our best pike fishing with fly rods has been sight fishing. Monster pike linger in shallow water after spawning. A few years ago Craig and I went to Phelps Lake together. Now both grown men, we yelled and hollered as we cast to 40 inch pike cruising in less than five feet of water. A carefully cast four or five inch streamer made of zonker strips, I call them black bunnies, rarely got past one of the huge pike we saw. As the fly approached a fish, it simply disappeared. And the battle would be on, powerful runs, thrashing on the surface. What's not to like?

My long-time enthusiasm for pike fishing still extends to the modest-sized fish found in Carpenter Lake, and many other lakes in Michigan, Wisconsin, and elsewhere. After a trip to Ontario where Craig and I caught much larger pike, we stopped at the cabin in Michigan. There we were catching pike between 20 and 25 inches and having a high time. I noted the irony that a week ago we were shaking pike that size off. Craig, still a teenager, said, "Dad, this is what the lake can give us."

In the last few years on the small lakes I fish in Michigan, I have fished for pike from my tube boat with my 8 weight. In half a day, I can paddle myself once around Carpenter Lake. As is true everywhere I ever fished, sometimes things are pretty slow. More frequently, however, I have steady action on the two to five pound pike in the lake.

A couple of months ago, fishing in Ontario, I hooked a two foot pike. As I was bringing it to the boat, my companion noted it was a little one. I replied, and this is one of the basic truths of my life, "Pike that size are the fish of my youth. The day I catch a pike like that and it's not a great thing will be a very sad day."

Ultimately I gave up the dream of playing first base for the Detroit Tigers. But the lure, the fascination, with pike fishing lingers on. And I call myself fortunate.

From the mountain top, we could hear Thoreau's wind of creation.

Chapter 12
Journey to Cold Mountain

"The morning wind forever blows, the poem of creation is uninterrupted; but few are the ears that hear it." At least, so thought Henry David Thoreau, the philosopher of Walden Pond, as he wrote in the mid-1850s.

Thoreau's Walden Pond has been overtaken by Concord, Massachusetts. To find his place of seclusion, his spot where he could go to hear sounds of the morning wind that few others heard, the wind that reminded him of creation, Thoreau only went a few miles from town. Today a few miles are not enough.

Any of us who want to hear the morning wind unblemished by the rush of trucks on the Interstate or the Saturday morning roar of lawnmowers need to go further, take more pains with our trek.

One summer my then teenage son, Craig, Dr. Larry Barden of the Biology Department at the University of North Carolina at Charlotte, and I went further, took more pains. When we reached our destination, there were few folks we might otherwise find wandering the shopping malls. In the morning, after a restful night in our sleeping bags, we heard the wind that few ears hear.

We hiked along Deep Gap Trail, a spur off the famous Art Loeb Trail in the Shining Rock Wilderness Area, up to Cold Mountain. The Shining Rock Wilderness Area is south of Canton, North Carolina, north of Brevard, and bordered on the east by the Blue Ridge Parkway.

Deep Gap Trail starts adjacent to the Little East Fork of the Pigeon River at the Daniel Boone Boy Scout Camp. The U. S. Forest Service, which maintains the Shining Gap Wilderness Area, allows parking at the base of the Trail. Given the character of the Trail, a major parking lot comparable to those at the shopping malls we left behind is not required.

The first quarter mile or so of the Deep Gap Trail is pretty steep. Craig and I had never been along this trail. We wondered if tried and true buddy Dr. Barden had mistaken us for mountain goats. After the rigorous start, however, the way evened out, though usually uphill a little. Periodically we crossed a small ravine, sometimes with a dry bottom, but more frequently with a small stream pouring down the mountain side. The rain which fell on the east coast filled not only the ponds of the Piedmont but the streams of the hills. These streams were clear, cold, and tumbling over the rocks.

We went through ever changing forest. According to what ecologists know as Hopkins Bioclimactic Law, 1000 feet of change in elevation is equivalent to a 100 mile change in latitude. As we marched up the mountain side from the 3000 feet at Daniel Boone Camp to the peak of Cold Mountain at 6030 feet, we went through several different plant communities.

At the lowest level, the predominant forest type was the oak-hickory community. Larry explained to us at one time this forest was marked by huge American Chestnut trees. In the 1890s chestnut blight, a fungus, was brought to the United States, probably by accident, from the Orient. The blight spread rapidly. It virtually eliminated the American Chestnut as a canopy tree. We saw examples of shrub-like Chestnuts. Larry explained the blight attacked mature trees while the roots survived. In turn, the roots send up new shoots which grow into small trees. Unfortunately, the spores of the blight land on the developing tree and the fungus claims another victim.

At higher elevations, we passed through forests marked by Eastern Hemlock, a species I knew from my youth in Michigan. Indeed, shortly after our trip to Cold Mountain, Craig and I stood among the hemlocks at the spot where I first learned to identify them.

At the summit, we were in a transition zone, one of the southernmost outposts of the Boreal Forest, the dominant ecosystem of Canada. Larry explained Cold Mountain was one of the Appalachian Heath Balds gradually being reclaimed by forest. Research by ecologists suggests the balds were not natural but caused by human disturbance. Typically a combination of fire and agriculture cleared the forest. Once the areas were cleared of trees, the annual use of the meadows by grazing cattle and sheep kept the trees from recolonizing the sites. In most places, the balds are now being reclaimed by the forest, particularly in spots protected from further human disturbance. In the Great Smoky National Park several of the balds are being preserved by the Park Service as examples of this particular ecosystem.

At the peak of Cold Mountain, however, the forest is gradually reclaiming the meadows. Yet we did find open spots, and what remarkable spots they were. We pitched our tent a few yards from one about the size of a football field. It was aflame with wild flowers. Hundreds of Black-Eyed Susans, a native orchid, wild onions, wild carrots, and more I could not identify. In addition, we picked a nice mess of blueberries to bring home. Though spring is widely regarded as the peak for wildflowers, during our two days across the diverse ecosystems we saw at least 100 species in bloom.

In addition to the more common plants I could identify (or more correctly, that Larry could help me identify) there were numerous exotic species. Among the most interesting was an Indian Pipe, a plant I knew from Michigan. Indian Pipe is a member of the wintergreen family. It stands several inches high, often in clusters of five or six. Each stalk has a single drooping off-white terminal flower. It is not green, as most plants are, because it does not capture the sun's energy. It is a parasite feeding off the roots of others. The host does the hard work of photosynthesis while the Indian Pipe extracts sugars from the labor of others. Indian Pipes are found on the moist and shady forest floor. Further, the Shining Rock Wilderness Area includes five species of Rhododendron and two of Mountain Laurel. We were there after the peak for these, but we did see a few blossoms.

Designated wilderness under the Wilderness Act of 1964, the Shining Rock Wilderness Area is off-limits to roads, utility lines, off-road vehicles, and chain saws. We practiced "leave no trace camping." What we carried in, we carried out. Few tin cans mar the landscape. We did find some human detritus, plastic candy wrappings for example. Unless those of us who appreciate the wilderness, or for that matter public parks in teeming cities, take care not to leave litter behind soon the wilderness will no longer be wild.

From the parking lot to Deep Gap was a little over four miles. Along the Art Loeb Trail, we hiked to the top of Cold Mountain. From Deep Gap we descended a mild slope of half a mile or so, then a grade described on the U. S. Forest Service map as "steep." We did not need ropes and carabiners, but we all commented on the upgrade. By the time we reached the summit, we were covered with sweat.

All told, it took us about six hours to complete the hike in. We stopped periodically to have lunch, gaze across the increasingly distant valleys, or to consider the changing pattern of plant life. Hiking up the side of a mountain, with a backpack loaded with sleeping bags, cooking utensils, food, tent, cameras and whatnot is strenuous work. When we got to camp, we were all heated, though the temperature had dropped about 20^0 from the time we left Charlotte.

After we set up camp, we wandered across the summit. During the

1930s the Forest Service placed a metal marker indicating the highest point of Cold Mountain – 6030 feet. Rock outcroppings gave us a vista of broad valleys, narrow gaps, and distant peaks.

In the early light of morning, we had breakfast while clouds swirled about. This was the wind few hear. Sometimes we could see miles. Sometimes a few feet. Hot oatmeal, laced with fresh blueberries, sure tasted good and made a warm lump in our tummies. Somehow breakfast on the trail always tastes better.

We broke camp and reversed our route of yesterday. We did not take as many rest breaks, nor did Larry and I stop to study the plant life of the forest. Consequently, it did not take us as long to descend as it did to come up. Make no mistake, however, hiking down a trail which drops about 500 feet each mile is hard work. Craig started with his jacket, but by the end of the first mile he stuffed it into the top of his backpack.

Why would anyone hike a little over five miles up the side of the second highest peak in North Carolina, sleep on the ground, get up in the morning and hike back down? All the time carrying 30 or 40 pounds of gear?

To hear the wind Thoreau heard. The wind no one else can hear. At the top of Cold Mountain lots of people have been left behind. For lack of interest or whatever, most persons chose not to make the trek.

Wilderness areas offer something not found elsewhere. Some outdoor recreational activities can take place concurrently and adjacent to others. Those who want to picnic on wooden tables can do so while others swim in a nearby pool. Both picnicking and swimming in pools are fine things. I have done both and look forward to doing so again.

Some activities, however, are mutually exclusive. If one is done, it preempts others. Primitive hiking and camping cannot be done where off-road vehicles roam. In order to make such things possible, for those who want to hear Thoreau's wind of creation, restricted wilderness areas – like those at Cold Mountain – must be preserved.

After half a century, I caught a Lake St. Clair musky.

Chapter 13
Homer LeBlanc Redux

Homer LeBlanc was one of my boyhood heroes. While I was growing up in southern Michigan, a regular feature of our household was Mort Neff's TV show, "Michigan Outdoors." Homer LeBlanc appeared frequently on Neff's show, displaying huge muskies he caught on Lake St. Clair, just north of Detroit.

Big fish have excited me as long as I can remember and Dad said even longer than that. Lake St. Clair was about 150 miles from home. I often told Dad we ought to go to there and catch some of those trophy muskies.

We never made it and without a driver's license all I could do was dream about Homer LeBlanc, read magazine articles, and wait.

From LeBlanc's TV interviews and other accounts I knew he caught most muskies trolling, often with lures swirling in the prop wash only a few feet from the boat. Dad and I always trolled with long lines. I could not imagine how a trophy fish would get so close to a boat that a lure in the prop wash would catch one.

Gradually, the yearning to fish Lake St. Clair and emulate Homer LeBlanc lessened. Yet, the recollections never faded. LeBlanc and the giant muskies he caught were wedged in some corner of my memory.

In early September, 2001, those recollections were suddenly brought to the surface when I got a chance to fish for muskies with Marc Thorpe on the Ottawa River north of Montreal, Quebec. After a day or so in Marc's boat, I said, "Trolling the way you do, with a couple of lures just off the corners of the boat and others in the prop wash, reminds me of Homer LeBlanc and the way he fished Lake St. Clair."

With a look of mild astonishment, Marc replied, "Oh, I'm a follower of Homer LeBlanc. I've got his book and it's all marked up. That's where I learned to fish the way I do."

Could have blown me away! Here was someone who had heard of Homer LeBlanc, followed his methods, and told me about a book I never knew existed. It took a while, yet with extensive internet searches and correspondence with used book stores in the Detroit area, I found a copy of *Homer LeBlanc, Muskie Fishing: Fact and Fancy, Lore and Lures.*

LeBlanc's book was not a literary masterpiece. It was a collection of fishing insights, jokes, observations about the frailties of persons and fish, and aphorisms. Some of these were of dubious utility, for example the assertion, "To be a Muskie fisherman, the smell of a Muskie is like the fragrant smell of perfume from a beautiful, shapely woman." That's a proposition I would not dare make just before we went out to dinner.

LeBlanc's trolling method was scattered throughout the book. Michigan law when LeBlanc fished permitted two rods per angler. With four persons in his boat, LeBlanc could use eight rods in holders. Toward the bow, LeBlanc rigged 10 foot, hollow glass rods and trolled with 75 feet of line out. These rigs often had a two ounce or three ounce keel sinker.

Amidships on both sides were four and a half or five foot rods, angled toward the stern. On these rods, enough line was released to position the lures a few feet from the stern and running a couple of feet deep. At the stern corners, two more rods, about five feet long, were perpendicular to the gunnels. About 30 feet of line was used with these rods. Two more rods were positioned directly astern, pointing down toward the water. Lures off these rods were only 15 feet behind the boat, on either side of the prop wash.

With this setup, LeBlanc could troll with no lure closer than 10 feet to another. Because some of the lures were very close to the boat, LeBlanc could change directions without tangling lines. He noted many of his competitors who tried the multiple rod method spent lots of time unraveling lines because they used too much line.

Marc Thorpe used only four rods. Yet, the overall system was comparable to the one developed by LeBlanc. One rod was set off the stern and line released until the lure was about 75 feet behind the boat. At the opposite corner, Marc positioned a second rod. On this rig, the lure was only 15 or 20 feet behind the boat. If the plug was brightly colored, it could often be seen a couple of feet below the surface. Two other rods were located at the stern. The lures were in the prop wash, one 15 or 20 feet behind the boat and the other 30 or 40 feet astern.

Marc did not guess how much line was out. LeBlanc recommended, "…when letting out a lure, don't throw it into the water, lay it in and expect a strike RIGHT NOW. [Capitalization in the original.] Watch the lure work for a few seconds." Each time Marc put a lure in the water in the three days I fished with him, he watched it carefully to be sure it worked properly before letting out more line. He stripped line off the reel and counted how many lengths of line were released. The distances I have given were ranges. Marc adjusted the distance on each rig according to his judgment how fish were hitting and what was likely to work with different lures and locations.

LeBlanc fished at varied depths. Particularly early in the morning he liked to run lures close to the bottom. To control the depth of his lures,

LeBlanc relied on varied weight keel sinkers.

Marc believed there were deep fish and shallow fish. The deep water fish, he thought, were perhaps four feet deep over 60 feet of water. Shallow water fish may be very shallow. Marc said, "Most people fish below the fish. They run lures too deep. People would be surprised how shallow I catch fish." Much of the time I fished with Marc the lures were visible from the boat.

Marc had a method of taking lures deep not available to LeBlanc. Marc had self-tapping brass inserts positioned near the head of selected crankbaits. CD Divers and Big M's were examples. Marc screwed weights into lures which varied from half an ounce to two or three ounces. While increased depth was an important part of the weights fastened into the lures, Marc said greater lure stability was a more critical factor. Generally speaking, Marc used heavier weights close to the boat and lighter weights farther from the boat.

LeBlanc used single strand, stainless steel wire leaders. They were the best available in the 1950s. Marc used 200 pound test fluorocarbon leaders. They were about four feet long. Fluorocarbon, Marc said, lasts a couple of years. The snaps and swivels, Marc replaced every month.

While LeBlanc used monofilament line, certainly an innovation at the time, Marc used dacron on two rods and wire on the other two.

In the many years I trolled for pike and walleyes with Dad, he often asked, "Are you getting the wiggle?" What he wanted to know was whether my lure was operating at the optimum speed. LeBlanc said the standard trolling speed was four miles per hour. Wind or other conditions, LeBlanc granted, would cause a variation in boat speed.

Marc trolled a little faster. He also had better control of his speed than either Dad or LeBlanc. When I fished with Marc, his depth finder also displayed boat speed. We started trolling at 4.8 miles per hour and ranged up to 5.8 miles per hour. All the fish we caught, pike and muskies alike, were caught at these speeds. We tried both slower and faster, but these were the productive speeds.

No factor was more important to LeBlanc in determining the best lure color than an angler's confidence in a lure. He wrote, "If a certain lure or color has caught a few fish, you will almost always have it in the water… that's the lure you'll catch the most fish with." Specifically, LeBlanc recommended dark frog with red and yellow spots, orange with black and yellow spots, bass, perch, red and white, and black and white – all colors contemporary musky anglers know well.

Marc said lure color selection was partly a function of water clarity and partly a function of experience. Experience, of course, was analogous to LeBlanc's confidence. Green and black were among the most common lure colors when I fished with Marc. Black presented a good profile for muskies. "Black," Marc said, "is an easy way to trick fish as far as the profile is concerned. Though white is probably just as good." Marc preferred natural colors over prism or reflective colors. We used many perch-suggestive colors and every musky angler knows muskies like perch.

LeBlanc must have been a tinkerer. He invented three lures. One was a spoon with a bucktail on the hook called a Swim Zag. Another, the 4-B Spinner, was an in-line spinner that contemporary musky anglers call a bucktail. As far as I can determine, the Swim Zag and 4-B Spinner are only collector's items. The third lure, the Swim Whiz, was described by LeBlanc as platypus-shaped. It was plastic and had two line ties, one for trolling deep and one for trolling shallow. The Swim Whiz is still available. Marc had no interest in inventing lures.

For me, I was surprised to find someone who knew the work of Homer LeBlanc and could convince me of its merits. And I was both amazed and delighted to see big fish caught in the prop wash of a moving boat. I'll have to try that.

Shortly after an article appeared in *Esox Angler*, a magazine no longer published, about my trip with Marc I got an email from Kevin Backus who introduced himself as Homer LeBlanc's grandson. Backus is now among the elite muskie guides on Lake St. Clair. He follows his grandfather's methods to a T. And, Backus added, he would be delighted to take me fishing for muskies on Lake St. Clair. Who says boyhood dreams don't come true?

Backus began fishing with his grandfather at an early age. He said, "I caught my first muskie when I was two or three years old. By the time I was 10, I was kind of burned out on fishing. Going out with Grandpa

Homer LeBlanc's grandson, Keven Bacus, honors his granddad with the name of his boat.

was just a big boat ride. But after Grandpa died in 1993, I began fishing muskies again. And I just did all the things he taught me." Backus named his boat "Mr. Muskie Too" to emphasize following in his grandfather's tradition.

I met Kevin early one morning. We started the day repeating LeBlanc's "muskie prayer." It goes, "Dear Lord, may we catch a muskie so big that when telling about it, we will have no need to lie. Bring us back safely with our limit of muskie per each, especially since we will be fishing with Homer LeBlanc tackle. Amen."

As Kevin was rigging gear, I noticed one of the Swim Whiz lures he was tying on had "Homer LeBlanc Tackle" molded into the plastic. When I commented it was one of the original LeBlanc lures, he said, "Sure it is. My grandpa would roll over in his grave if he knew I was not using the lures he gave me. He did not give me this stuff for me to build a shrine. It was to go fishing and that's what I do. I can honor Grandpa more by using his lures than by setting them aside."

Kevin made no excuses for using his grandfather's methods. "Homer was not a millionaire," he said, "but he lived like one. I figured he may be on to something." Kevin has his grandfather's original maps of Lake St. Clair. He said, "Grandpa was about the first to chart Lake St. Clair. He spent thousands of hours with a weight on a line, dropping it over the side to measure the depth." Kevin now has his grandfather's trolling runs stored on a GPS/depth finder.

One of Kevin's grandfather's rules was, "Think like a muskie." He wrote, "To catch a big muskie, you fish hard and think like a muskie. I'm often asked, how do you think like a muskie? I answer, fishes [sic] don't have any brains [obviously not biologically true], and so it shouldn't be too hard to think like a muskie."

Out with Kevin, I caught six muskies, one close to 20 pounds. Not with Homer LeBlanc, but about as close to it as possible, I finally realized a boyhood dream, to catch Lake St. Clair muskies using the method taught by Homer LeBlanc.

The plane with a broken right wing, sitting in the rain, marking our night stranded in the Alaskan backcountry.

Chapter 14
Stranded

Neither Craig, Caleb, nor I anticipated we would be stranded. But we were.

It started normally enough as the float plane lifted off the Naknek River near King Salmon, Alaska. Craig, my son and long-time fishing buddy, Caleb Hitzfield, our guide, and I were on our way to Moraine River. We flew about 50 miles and landed on Crosswinds Lake. As the plane descended toward the small lake, whitecaps were clearly visible. As the pontoons hit the water, the plane bounced off a particularly nasty wave. When the plane came to a stop on the north shore of the lake, Caleb asked us, "You want to fish in this wind? Or go back?" The wind, as classified by meteorologists, was a moderate gale – inconvenience in walking – in the mid-30 mile-per-hour range.

Craig and I looked at one another. "We're already here. Let's go fishing." We unloaded our gear and started our mile walk to the Moraine River. Supposed to be monster rainbow trout at the Moraine River.

After checking the pontoons to determine whether they were damaged in the landing, the pilot turned the plane and headed downwind. In the 30 plus years I have been riding in float planes, I have seen many pilots maneuver planes in stiff wind. They fire the engine and drift slowly across the lake, tail downwind, until they are positioned for a take-off. This time, however, the pilot rotated the plane and went nose with the wind. Doing so meant he would have to turn again to take off into the wind. As the plane headed downwind, I thought, "I never saw that before." Later Craig, Caleb and eventually the pilot all recalled comparable reservations.

When the plane reached the southern end of the lake, the pilot began to turn left to get the nose into the wind. Gale-force winds caught the upwind wing and tipped the plane onto its side, rolling the cabin under water. Craig and Caleb dropped their gear and began running toward the southern end of the lake. Craig's hat took off tumbling along the ground and I started after his hat; after all, his mother and I gave him the hat when he was still in high school.

The right wing hit the bottom, preventing the plane from rolling completely over. Then the air-filled pontoon sought the surface. The plane popped upright and slowly drifted to the shore. Three feet of the right wing was broken and stuck up in the air at a rakish angle. By the time we got to the plane, the pilot was standing on the ground. Shaken, perhaps even stirred, but OK.

No taking off in that plane. The pilot started walking toward a US Park Service encampment a couple of miles away to radio for a rescue. Craig, Caleb and I headed toward the river to fish.

Fishing was tough! Temperatures were in the mid-40s. Most of the day we fished in rain. All day we were fishing in extreme wind. Straight casting was almost impossible. We used roll casts, flipping our weighted plastic salmon egg imitations into the current. Where there were rocks in the rapids, spray was whipped flat. Periodically, wind lifted water off the surface. Craig caught several nice rainbow trout. Best I could do was lose several, including one when Caleb told me, "Don't let him go any further downstream. We don't want that fish to jump opposite the bear on the far bank. We don't want the bear to try to catch the same fish we are trying to catch."

About 3:00 I asked Caleb, "What are the chances we will get picked up?"

He answered, "Oh, I think they'll come and get us. But we need to be at the lake by 4:00, even though the pick-up time is 4:30. If they come early, we want to be sure to be there." I agreed and we began our hike back to the lake about 3:30. Once we came out of the narrow valley of the river

There were bears wandering about where we spent the night in the wounded plane.

118

and onto the flat plain, walking was more difficult than it had been in the morning. We reached the meteorologic standard of fresh gale with winds gusting into the mid-40 mile-per-hour range. Caleb led and Craig and I walked close enough behind him and one another to take advantage of him breaking the wind.

Once at the lake, we clambered down a small bluff, perhaps half a dozen feet from the crest to the lake. It was 4:05. Other anglers were to the west of us, and they gathered small sticks for a fire. Craig, Caleb and I found spots in the grass and sat down to wait for our pick up. The plane that had brought us in was tied to the bank where the bluff above the lake was about 20 feet high. While we were protected, in a relative sense, from the wind, it nonetheless whipped around us. The lake was being beaten to a froth by the gale.

After a couple of brief dozes, at 5:00 I told Craig and Caleb I was getting cold and that I was going to climb into the wrecked plane. Both assured me it was just as cold in the plane as out. "Ah," I answered, "but I'll be out of the wind." The protection of the plane made a difference.

About 6:00, Craig joined me in the plane. He quickly noted it was more comfortable in the plane than on the bluff bank. Craig had been watching "Survivorman" on the Discovery Channel. Following the advice of the Survivorman, Craig took off his waders, tried to dry out his fleece pants and socks. In another hour, I followed suit; I should have done it when I first got in the plane.

In another hour, Caleb climbed in the plane. He suggested we crack a window lest we consume all the oxygen in the cabin. I told him there were enough places where the wind was coming in that we had plenty of air exchange. We ate some of our granola bars, drank some water, and waited. It was still plenty light for planes to function.

Another party of anglers had seven persons, including the guide. The pilot for that group radioed to the air base to ask for another plane. He thought, given the wind, that his group should be divided. Caleb, hanging around to get the latest word, asked the pilot to request a couple of sandwiches and sleeping bags when the second plane came in. Caleb came to our plane to say he expected we would spend the night in the bush.

By 8:00, the second plane arrived, complete with sandwiches and sleeping bags. When Caleb brought the sleeping bags, I claimed one without question. Historically, I get cold before anyone else, and I could anticipate the night in the plane would be cold. I was sitting in the pilot's seat with my feet stretched diagonally into the area below the passenger seat. Not an ideal posture, but the only one available. I draped the sleeping bag into position and stuffed my feet into the bottom. These were top quality bags with wind barriers along the zipper.

I told Caleb if I ever started a "scrounging" group I would name him as "head scrounger." He saved our bacon!

Craig took the second sleeping bag after Caleb said he would sleep in his waders in the storage compartment of the cabin.

Periodically, planes landed and took off. But our pick-up did not come.

About 9:00 we settled in with the expectation of sleeping the best we could. I had my fleece pants and jacket on. With the hood pulled around my head, I leaned against the window and went to sleep. From time-to-time during the night, we were awakened by wind tilting the plane – would the wind tip us over? The broken wing creaked in the wind all night long. Not a restful sleep.

At the northeast corner of the lake a group of seven French, three women and four men, was camped. They have been coming to the same spot for six years to photograph bears. During the evening, wind began to blow their tents down. They spent the night, outside in the wind and rain, sleeping in their sleeping bags. We thought we had it rough!

Shortly after 6:00 the leader of the French group came to offer us some granola bars and a cup of coffee. Coffee! Nectar of the gods! I waded along the edge of the lake toward their encampment. I explained to them that at one time I spoke French but that now I was just a student. Several noted that I could carry on conversation, in any event. They laughed when I said that I could ask where the WC was.

Caleb asked if their camp was ever bothered by bears. "No," they said, "though the bears sometimes wander along the ridge, about 50 yards away. Like those right there." Moments later, three different bears began to wander down the center of the small swale where they were camped. The bears retreated, however, when several folks began yelling at them.

We made our way back to the wrecked plane.

Wind still whipped the lake. At 10:00 a plane arrived to take us out. It was the same pilot as the one who brought us in. He said he flew over the lake about 8:00 the evening before but adjudged it was too windy to attempt to take us out.

Once we were loaded in the plane, he backed downwind and took off in due course. In an hour we were back at the airbase and headed to the lodge. Craig and I went for the adventure. But stranded in the bush all night was a little more than we had anticipated.

Chapter 15
Tents

Outdoor folk like tents, at least lots of outdoor folk do. There are many, I suspect, who think of themselves as outdoor folk who cringe at the notion of sleeping in a tent. A former student once sent me a questionnaire including a query about my favorite place to sleep. When I responded, "In my tent," she admonished me, "Dr. Mead, that's not what you were supposed to answer." She also challenged coffee as my favorite drink.

Cowboys and Indians

My first tent was four feet by four feet, I suspect four feet high, with a cowboy riding a bucking bronco on one side and an Indian chief in full-feathered headdress on the other. No floor, just the ground.

One summer, it must have been 1947 as Nancy was a toddler and in 1948 we made a family trip to the UP, we were staying at the house in Arcadia, Michigan. While I was born in Uncle Bill's and Aunt Eva's house a couple of blocks away, the house on Second Street is the one I remember. We lived there until I was three years old and left in 1941. I had my tent set up in the yard beside the house.

It came time to go to bed and I said I wanted to sleep in my tent. Before Mom could enter an objection, Dad said, "You want to sleep in the tent? Go get the tent and we'll go out to the lake and sleep on the beach. I'll get everything else." The lake he meant was Lake Michigan. I hustled to take down the tent and load it in the back of the Model T.

Dad drove south of town and turned up the road to Chamberlain's dairy. Then past Chamberlain's to the end of the road, perhaps 100 yards from Lake Michigan. Dad turned off the lights on the car and I said, to

Dad's amusement for the next 60 years, "Wow, it's dark out here."

We carried our gear to the beach. I suspect Dad carried and I merely tagged along. Dad dug out a small depression in the sand and we set up the tent over it. We did not have any sleeping bags, just blankets. And I went promptly to sleep.

Dad had a rugged night. He stuck out of the tent a couple of feet, though I doubt that made much difference to his sleep.

In the morning, Dad gathered driftwood, made a fire and cooked eggs for breakfast. Mom and Dad had a couple of frypans with thin metal bottoms and retrospectively I suspect were difficult to cook with. Dad used one of those pans to cook the eggs.

The Canvas Monstrosity

In 1948, we had a new car. Dad put his name in to an Oldmobile dealer in Lansing during World War II. Folks there told him there were

This canvas tent was heavy, but it served the family well. Dad and Mom discussing something. The green Oldsmobile suggests late 1950s.

no cars for sale and Oldsmobile was now making trucks for the war effort. Once the war was over, however, Dad's name was among the first to get a car – a two tone, two-door, brown sedan.

That summer, we headed out. First we went to Arcadia where Uncle Bill convinced Dad a drive up the east side of Lake Superior to the Montreal River where the road ended would be a nice trip. I can remember asking Uncle Bill if Canadian trout would eat worms. He speculated they would.

For the trip, Dad bought a tent from Curley Fetters. It was canvas, top and bottom. It was an umbrella tent with a central post and four arms off the post extending to the corners. And heavy. Using it later, I estimated it weighed 75 pounds including the posts and stakes. Not a backpacker's tent.

Where all we camped, I cannot remember. One of the places was the Dead River Storage Basin outside Marquette. (See Chapter 3, "The Big Ones Get Away.")

Another place we camped on the trip to the UP was Lake Gogebic State Park. Dad got advice on fishing the lake from someone, probably the Conservation Officer at the Park. We trolled for walleyes using June Bug spinners, heavy bass-style weights, and minnows. I still have my June Bug spinner.

We caught enough walleyes for dinner. One of Dad's was over 20 inches. I got one with an aluminum tag on its lip. It had been stocked by what was then the Department of Conservation. The Park Ranger came by to check on whatever Rangers check and he took the number off the tag but left the tag with me. *In-Fisherman* reported many years later on the difficulty of assessing stocking with tagged fish and listed only three walleyes from Lake Gogebic in 1948; my tag was one of the three. I no longer have the tag.

At Lake Gogebic I was let in on my first adult secret. We would celebrate Nancy's fifth birthday on September 4th, not the 5th. On the 5th, we would be crossing Lake Michigan from Marinette, Wisconsin to Frankfort, Michigan. I was told never to tell. But now I have given up the secret.

In the early 1950s we established our camp at the cabin in the UP. (See Chapter 2, "The Cabin.") It became, and remains, a central spot in the family's outdoor experience. From Springport, where we lived, a trip to the cabin was a major enterprise. Not a long weekend trip, particularly before Big Mac, the bridge between the Lower and the Upper Peninsulas, was constructed.

At some point, I was probably 15 or 16, I said there were lots of places we could go where there was good trout fishing and we could camp out. Mom and Dad challenged me to find some. So, I did.

One of the places I found was a CCC camp on the Pigeon River, outside Wolverine, Michigan. We went there several times. On one of the trips, as we sat around the camp fire after dinner, a Whip-poor-will began to call. I answered. Mom, Dad, and Nancy were quiet. The fire by now was merely coals. The bird and I kept calling one another. He got closer and closer. Finally, he landed in front of the tent, saw he had made a terrible mistake and took off.

Most of what follows, I was told. I slept. The canvas tent had no rain-fly. The tent kept off the rain and it did pretty well. Dad and I slept on the ground on one side of the tent and Mom and Nancy slept on cots on the other side of the tent. Whoever came in the tent last did not fasten the door flap. It poured. All the rain collected on the front of the tent sluiced onto the floor and accumulated. Dad, on the floor and closest to the center of the tent realized he was sleeping in a puddle. He got up, rustled about, and asked me for help. I remember that. I dug through my pants pocket, gave him my jackknife and went back to sleep. Dad commandeered Nancy's cot and had her stretch out across the bottom of the two cots. The episode proved the bottom of the tent did not leak.

On another trip to the CCC camp, Dad and I came back from fishing and Mom said she found a trail but did not want to take it alone. So, Mom and I began walking along what was clearly an established trail. We were not talking much, just moving along quietly. We came to an opening in the forest and there were four deer, three does and a buck. We stood very still. The buck snorted. And two of the does leapt for the woods. The third doe moved cautiously in our direction, staring right at us. The buck came between us and the doe and snorted again. The two does already in the woods went further. The third doe stood her ground. The mosquitoes were eating us alive. Mom moved to swat one and the buck snorted and all ran into the woods. Remind anyone of Feline, Bambi's aunt?

When I was in graduate school Mom made the hike again. She picked up a small piece of birch bark, wrote on it, "Dear Tim, we didn't go far enough to see the pure white birches you and I saw but got some bark from some very nice ones. Never have I been so impressed by anything. Love, Mom." I put the sliver of bark between two plastic sheets. The message is badly faded. I still have it.

We got lots of use from the canvas tent. For a while I used it after we got to North Carolina. Finally I asked Nancy Bond if she wanted it for sentimental reasons. When she said she did not want it, I discarded it. The value in the tent was in the memories it created.

The Dome Tent

In 1985 I went to Ontario's Quetico Provincial Park as Larry Barden's travel partner. Heinz and Elisabeth Feil went with us. Larry had a Eureka Timberline A-frame tent. It was light and easy to carry. Easy to set up and take down. I knew I had to get a backcountry camping tent. I kept my eye out.

The Great Outdoor Provision Company in Charlotte was moving to new location at the Park Road Shopping Center. Among the items on the introductory sale was a Eureka Wind River. I went to check it out. Nice enough tent, but not an A-frame. A dome tent.

But the price was right, so I bought it. Turned out, it was a great buy. I came to believe a dome tent superior to an A-frame. In 1991, Craig and I were camped at McDougall Lake in Quetico Park with Larry and Larry's son, Jeff. A terrible wind storm came up (for more details, see, "Storms Over Quetico," in my other book, *Quetico Adventures*). The wind laid the dome tent flat against Craig and me, huddled in it for protection. When the wind subsided, the tent snapped back into its original shape. Larry's A-frame, however, had bent poles not repairable in the back country.

The Wind River served many years of trips into Quetico Park. I slept in the tent in Ontario, Michigan, Montana, Ohio, North Carolina, South

The Wind River tent worked great until it just gave up. Wayne Harrison is pondering the lake.

Carolina, and probably a couple more I cannot recall. It never leaked. It was spacious enough for two persons, with a little space left over for shoes and the like during the night. I suspect I amortized the cost to about fifty cents a night. That does not include the cost of getting to the places I pitched the tent.

In 2014, I came back to camp and saw two long tears in the rainfly. I repaired the tears with duck tape. But I could see the Wind River was coming to the end of its useful life. Rips caused by the wind were merely a symptom of the aged tent's demise. But I loved that tent.

For Truck Camping

Bill Shumaker has been a frequent victim of my notions to go somewhere fishing. On our first trip to Montana, we slept in the back of the truck, moving gear each night and morning from the back to the cab. Clever guys, we decided to take a tent and stash gear in the tent while we slept in the truck. Even more clever, we slept in the tent and did not move gear at all. Bill's tent served the purpose for all the years Bill travelled to Montana with me.

When Bill decided to skip the Montana trip, I needed a tent. I bought a Coleman dome tent. It's light enough, I suspect, to serve as a back country tent for some folks, but it's too heavy for me. For truck camping, it's ideal. Coleman claims it sleeps four and it could if all four were willing to crowd. For two, it has lots of space. Even when I have traveled to Montana alone, or camped other spots when I was traveling by truck rather than Shank's Mare, it has been a super tent.

Replacing the Wind River

When the next trip to Quetico Park loomed after deciding the Wind River could not make another trip, I needed a tent. Folks who know me will be surprised at this; I shopped around.

Though more expensive than some tents. I selected a REI Half Dome. My first trip with it was with Hank Oates (see Chapter 19, "It Was a Yummy Trip," in *Quetico Adventures*). Like the Wind River, it was a dome tent with sufficient space for two guys and a little gear. It has large space under the rain fly but outside the tent for shoes and other detritus. The poles and the places they go are color-coded so even dodos like me can pitch the tent.

The last time I used it, in Quetico Park with Mike Quinn, we broke one of the poles. With Mike's ingenuity, we fashioned a support for the broken pole with a stick selected for length and some wraps to keep it in place. When I got home, I ordered new poles.

Solo

For some time I have admired solo travelers in the wilderness, folks who go off by themselves and take the risks of being in the backcountry alone. There are risks, but the reward is the solitude which goes with being alone. I've done some of that when in Montana and I did not have a companion at Rock Creek or one of the other remote places I have camped. But I also had a tent I used for two campers. So, I have coveted a solo tent.

REI sent a flier to members. Tent sale. And I had a $100 credit at REI. Plus, as an REI member, I got 10% back in credit at the end of the year. I went to the local REI outlet, looked at tents and bought a Quarter Dome.

In the first year I had it, I used it once. I loaded my gear and went to the primitive camping area at North Carolina's South Mountains State Park. The primitive camping area is at the top of the mountain, a hike up the hill of a couple of miles and a significant change in elevation. Hard to make the case the area is really remote. Mountain bikers come through. Other hikers and campers come through. The night I spent there I was visited by a hound with two radio collars; a bear hunter's dog, I suspect, who was on his own.

In 2016, I used the one-person tent on a solo trip to Quetico Park (see Chapter 28, "Alone, but Not Lonely") and in the trip in the Montana high country for golden trout (see Chapter 21, "A Golden Opportunity).

Coda

Are tents as much fun messing with as boats? Can't answer that one. Yet, tents over my life have played a critical role in making possible the things I really like to do. Sleeping on the ground and listening to the rain on the fly stand alone as a key satisfaction. Hope it rains tonight.

Chapter 16
Wilderness, Thoreau and Me

Wilderness. It conjures up different things, depending on each individual's perspective. For some, wilderness is the trackless desert of the southwest. For some, wilderness is the urban jungle. Neither, of course quite catches the truth. The desert is not trackless nor are cities jungles. For me, wilderness is the boreal forest stretching across North America from ocean to ocean. In my version of wilderness, there are no roads, no conveniences, few people.

One year as spring semester wound down, a student familiar with my wilderness adventures asked, "Dr. Mead, are you going to Canada again this year?"

I answered, "As soon as commencement is over, don't get between me and my truck. I'm getting outta here." Most students did not know of my trips to the forest, so I took a few minutes to explain. One student asked how I took a shower. I replied, "I bathe in the lake. There's no shower for 70 miles in any direction."

A young woman, sitting right next to the lectern, muttered to herself, "I wouldn't go where there was no shower for 70 miles."

Yet, despite my student's view, wilderness is not hostile. A number of years ago I watched a TV documentary about the life of the arctic fox. The narrator referred often to the "hostile environment" and how the fox struggled to survive. Deep snow existed much of the year making mice and other prey hard to catch. Yet, for the fox, this was the best environment. That's why the arctic fox lived there rather than in downtown Los Angeles. On the trip to the Sutton River, Len Anderson and I saw an arctic fox (see Chapter 22, "Sutton River"). It was a highlight of our trip.

In part, the appeal of wilderness for me springs from summers in

Michigan's Upper Peninsula. In the early 1950s Mom and Dad purchased land near Lake Superior and built a cabin there (see Chapter 2, "The Cabin"). In my teens I wandered through the forest. Once, while still in high school, I awoke before anyone else, slipped on my clothes and headed out. I saw fresh tracks along a dirt road and began to follow them along a deer trail skirting the edge of the lake. Suddenly, startling both of us, a buck jumped up a few feet ahead of me and crashed off through the underbrush. Wonderful.

Henry David Thoreau

In the years since, my appreciation of wilderness has grown with trips to outpost fishing camps in Ontario and Saskatchewan, float trips to Hudson Bay fishing for trophy brook trout and rainbow trout in Alaska, hiking and camping in the mountains of North Carolina and Montana, hiking in the desert of Arizona. No doubt my most significant wilderness experience has been in the 30 trips I have taken in Ontario's Quetico Provincial Park (see my book *Quetico Adventures* and Chapter 28 of this book, "Alone, But Not Lonely").

Wilderness travel has been important to me not only for the rich experiences but also for the values wilderness represents. These values have been captured in what some contend is the first environmental writing in the American canon, *Walden* by Henry David Thoreau. Carl Bode, an editor of Thoreau's work, called it the "greatest document" of the transcendentalist movement.

I first read *Walden* when I borrowed it from the high school library. During my undergraduate years, I wrote a term paper titled "Thoreau as a Social Critic." Certainly, there is plenty of social criticism in *Walden*. In the several semesters I taught an undergraduate course titled American Political Thought, I always fell behind the syllabus when I came to Thoreau and Emerson. I now own two or three copies of Thoreau's masterpiece, each marked and cross-referenced to other works or other passages.

Among the values, for me, of wilderness is captured by one of the most famous passages in *Walden*. In a chapter titled "Where I Lived, and What I Lived For," Thoreau urged, "Simplicity, simplicity, simplicity!" and later, "Simplify, simplify."

Life in the wilderness, in my experience, is pretty simple. Chores of the day, whatever they may be, dominate. To cook meals, gather firewood. To provide shelter, pitch the tent. It's not hard to figure out what needs to be done. In Thoreau's first chapter, titled "Economy," he said his experience at Walden Pond was marked by a "few implements," but, "Most luxuries, and many of the so-called comforts of life, are not only not indispensable, but positive hindrances to the elevation of mankind."

Thoreau said he went to Walden Pond, "...to live deliberately, to front only the essential facts of life...to live deep and suck out all the marrow of life." Thoreau's desire captures much of the attraction of wilderness to me. While there are periods of rest – I particularly enjoy an afternoon nap stretched out on a big, flat rock – most of the day is spent living, the tasks of being alive. Setting up camp, breaking camp, portaging, hiking, gathering fire wood, cooking the meals.

Wilderness travel provides a lab for me to identify, for myself, who I am. Each year and each trip into the bush requires me to test myself, to challenge myself in a way life in the city does not. When Hank Oates went to Quetico Park with me, he often asserted, "Not many people I know could do this."

Thoreau wrote, "I know of no more encouraging fact than the unquestionable ability of man to elevate his life by a conscious endeavor." Some folks do not need a personal challenge. I thrive on it.

Folks often tell me, "For your age…." (Disclaimer, as I type these words, I'm 78 and nearing 79.) My response usually is, "Most folks my age are dead." I'm not interested in being dead. I'm interested in being alive. I do not test myself against most people. I test myself against myself. It's clear, I cannot do what I did 20 years ago. A number of years ago, Hugh LeBlanc, who directed my doctoral dissertation, asked, "How many more times are you going to do this?"

I answered, "One too many."

Backcountry expeditions are a test of self-reliance. If the preparation is inadequate, no one to blame but myself. If the firewood is not collected, no one to blame but myself. Each successful trip is a test of self-reliance. Emerson's essay of that title has always been a favorite. I appreciate measuring myself against it. Which in turn leads to a sense of accomplishment. Yet, *Walden* is about more than self-reliance. It is about self-development.

When I head into the wilderness, lots of gear which might be useful gets left behind. Bare essentials, items I am pretty sure I will actually use, go with me. I am a list maker. Before I head into the wilderness, I check off items on my list as I pack. By now, my lists are well-established. If something is not on the list, it does not go. When I take folks with me, I send them a copy of my list, with an admonition, "Take this and nothing else." On three of my trips to Ontario's Quetico Provincial Park, my travel companions used my list only as a starting point. Mike Quinn, one of the three, lugged extra gear across every portage trail. I asked Mike to weigh, when he got home, the gear he did not use; it weighed 85 pounds.

One of the areas where I simplify is my fishing gear. In my bass boat, I carry multiple rods, hundreds of lures of varied colors, depth finders fore and aft. On my Sutton River brook trout trip (see Chapter 22, "Sutton River"), for example, I carried two fly rods and two reels, a couple of dozen flies and half a dozen leaders. On the trip to Sylvan Lake (see Chapter 21, "Golden Opportunity"), my flies were in a flat box, ¼ inch by three inches by four inches. This gear would have to work. If a companion started to catch trout on a fly I did not have, tough. Doubtless, without a lure to meet every possibility and no depth finders, I fish better. I have to read the bank, the current, and figure out how conditions determine how I can catch fish. Simplify, simplify.

In part, Thoreau's admonition to simplify was a reaction to the materialism of his age. (What would he think of me now as I pound the keys on my lap top?) In a famous line, he urged, "…beware of all enterprises that require new clothes." In contrast to Thoreau, my wilderness gear includes polypropylene underwear, fleece jackets, and Gore-Tex® rain gear, and other space age gear. Thoreau hoped to focus attention on the enterprise of life, not the costumes that sometimes overtake life itself.

Thoreau did not go to Walden Pond to be anti-social. Indeed, Thoreau's cabin was close enough to Concord he often wandered into town to have dinner with the Emersons. He had, he said, "…three chairs in my house, one for solitude, two for friendship, and three for society." Thoreau often had, he said, 25 or 30 guests and they stood.

In addition to my family, I have had multiple companions in the wilderness. Larry Barden often accompanied me to Quetico Park; indeed, Larry introduced me to Quetico. Hank Oates, Scott Van Horn, Eric Yarborough, John Altman, Bill Toole, Wayne Harrison and Mike Quinn accompanied me on wonderful trips to Quetico Park. Bill Shumaker made many trips to Montana with me. Mike Climer and Bob Martin joined me to fish Montana. My life has been enriched by them all.

What makes a good wilderness companion is not science (see Chapter 35, "Choosing Wilderness Travel Companions," *Quetico Adventures*). Personal compatibility is a factor, but not a *sine qua non*. A good sense of humor helps. A risk-averse perspective is a must. Lots of experience might be helpful, but is not a requirement if there is a willingness to learn and pitch in with tasks.

Among my favorite chapters in *Walden* is "Solitude." Thoreau reported he once felt lonesome in his early weeks at Walden Pond, but he soon overcame the feeling. During a rainstorm he, "…was suddenly sensible of such sweet and beneficent society in Nature…as made the fancied advantages of human neighborhood insignificant, and I have never thought of them since." He wrote, "I never found the companion that was so companionable as solitude." Much of Thoreau's perspective parallels that of Emerson's earlier seminal essay, *Nature*.

At Walden, Thoreau claimed he had two constant visitors. One was an old man who dug the pond and lined it with rocks and trees and that was Thoreau's god. The other was an old woman whom most never saw but in whose garden Thoreau learned the "original of every fable" of life and she was Nature.

Once as we prepared to enter Quetico Park someone from the Ely, Minnesota Chamber of Commerce interviewed Larry Barden and me. When asked what I valued about wilderness, I answered, "It was a place to be alone without being lonely" (see Chapter 28, "Alone, But Not Lonely").

For a number of years my observation lingered on the Chamber's brochure on wilderness travel near Ely. Often I have taken a cup of coffee to the edge of a lake or stream and remained there, quite alone, for hours. Or hiked through the forest and stood overlooking a beaver pond. Only the white noise of nature – the lapping of water at the lake's edge, the cry of a distant loon or the silver song of a lark seeking a companion, the splash of a trout in a pond – these have kept me company.

In the US, wilderness preservation reached an apogee with the passage of the Wilderness Act in 1964. The Act set aside 9.1 million acres of federal land where "...the earth and its community of life are untrammeled by man, where man himself is a visitor and does not remain." Such areas, according to the statute, shall be, "...without permanent improvements or human habitation."

Periodically there are attacks on wilderness lands. Particularly in western states political forces are trying to wrest land owned by the US government to state ownership. An element of the claim is that the land should be "returned" to the states. Of course, the national government owned the land before there were states or territories. Something cannot be returned to those who never had it. Unfortunately, the record of states in protecting public lands is not good. Often public lands have been sold to private interests – mining, agriculture, or private preserves – where public access has been lost. The Wilderness Society and Back County Hunters and Anglers have led the resistance to transfer of public lands to the states, and in the states there are a variety of comparable organizations.

Walden is not merely a chronology of some anti-social nut. It is a spiritual work which captures the core transcendental values of nature and humanity's place in it and responsibility for self. In the chapter titled "Spring," Thoreau says, "We need the tonic of wilderness." That's why I go to places with no shower for 70 miles. Wild places are my tonic, my source of personal renewal. *Walden* is not the reason I go to wilderness. But the rationale can be found there.

Chapter 17
Dog Sled Adventure

For years I have followed the Iditarod Sled Dog race in Alaska, a trek of more than a 1000 miles across the wilderness in the dead of winter. Started in 1973, the race honors dog sled teams which carried vaccine in 1925 from Anchorage to Nome during a diphtheria epidemic.

I recalled Ed Stielstra from McMillan, Michigan had run Iditarod. An internet search located Nature's Kennel where Ed and his wife Tasha offer novices dog sled trips. I signed up.

Breakfast was provided at the kennel. All the novice mushers got instruction in putting harnesses on the dogs. Tasha gave each novice a list of the dogs in "our" team. My team had Badger and Gretzky as the lead dogs. Art and Ontario were in the middle and brothers Tucker and Sakic were the "wheel dogs," that is the dogs closest to the sled. Iditarod teams start with 18 or 16 dogs. The novice units only had six dogs. We would run at roughly the same speed as Iditarod teams, however, 10 miles per hour.

Harnesses were color-coded for the size of the dogs. Badger, with a big, powerful chest, got a pink harness. Badger has run Iditarod four times and was clearly the boss of my team. During the runs, the dogs drank by licking up snow from the side of the trail. When Gretzky wanted to drink, he had to tug to get to the side of the trail. When Badger wanted to drink, he just moved the team to his side of the trail. Gretzky, Tucker and Sakic had red harnesses and Art and Ontario had blue ones.

When the dogs saw people with harnesses, they got excited. "Take me, take me!" they seemed to say. PETA to the contrary, these dogs were not abused when running! They hold their heads up, waiting for the harnesses. The sleds had to be tethered or the first couple of dogs would take off and leave the rest behind.

Then we went on a "puppy run." Johnnie had a team ready to go. He led and, one at a time, each dude followed. We went around a circular trail for ten minutes or so, acclimating ourselves to the sled and its operation. When we finished, we dismantled the team and put the dogs back in their individual spots. At the end of each run, the dogs got hugs and pats and "good dogs." They loved it. Badger was a little too sophisticated to show it, but he stood and looked up with a sort of "we did it, didn't we." Gretzky leaned up against my knees, hard.

Readying the team.

After all the teams were back at their spots, we went back in the lodge for lunch.

On a double piece of aluminum foil, about 2 feet by 20 inches, daubed with thick margarine, we put sliced potatoes, pieces of venison sausage, meat balls, vegetables, and spices. We wrapped the foil, sealing it all around. Dinner, to be cooked in the foil.

Then, we went back out to the kennel to re-rig our teams and start out on the trail. Each team was set up sequentially. A guide went first. Then the dudes. So, each of the couples had a guide and Tasha served as my guide. Each set of teams went off at twenty minute, or so, intervals. We wandered the roads and trails west and north of the kennel.

Riding behind a team of sled dogs was lots of fun. But it was no piece of cake. I got pitched from the sled six times in two days.

At a sharp corner, Tasha was looking back at me, taking pictures. How tough could it be? The wheel dogs cut it a little short – seemed, to me at least, they often do. The sled ran up on the snow piled at the edge of the trail. I was flying parallel to the ground. Thump! I landed at least 20 feet from the spot where the sled tipped. Tasha stopped the team. And that's why the guides preceded the dudes.

Twice more I got pitched. Once my team ran into Tasha's and she and her sled got tipped as well and the two teams dragged her along the ground before she could restore order. Tough lady!

Gretsky, eventually, turned back to look at me at each corner. It was not that he cared whether I was still there. He and the other dogs were going to keep running. He was curious, that's all.

What did I learn about staying on the runners? Well, watching Tasha wasn't adequate. At some of the spots where I wrecked, she was standing on the runners of her sled facing me.

So, here's what I think I learned. 1) Stay low. Got so I was squatting at trail corners while Tasha was standing. 2) Lean toward the inside of the turn. Counter the centrifugal force of the sled. 3) Don't go too fast. When you get thrown off going fast, you get hurled through the air. 4) Don't go too slow. When I slowed way down coming into a corner, the dogs pulled the sled into the snow piled up along the trail. And faster sled speed permitted the sled to skid out into the trail. But I still got pitched off the second day.

Once we completed our first day 20 miles, we came to a camp set up in the woods. Our first chore was to take the dogs from the sled and fasten them to the lines established for the purpose. There were three 50 yard cables stretched between posts sunk in the soil. Tasha and I were the last to arrive at camp, so our dogs were at the end of one of the cables.

Then we fed the dogs, frozen meat, chopped into small pieces, dumped into boiling water, along with dried kibble. This is the meal dogs get during Iditarod.

Dogs also got a bundle of straw to make a bed. Some of the dogs

Here I go, down the trail.

arranged the straw "just so." Others kicked it away. Within an hour or two, most of the dogs burrowed a hole into the packed snow. They slept in the burrows.

A central feature of the camp was an outfitters tent with a wood floor, several bunk beds and a wood stove. With the wood stove fired up it was probably in the upper 30 degrees F range in the tent.

A big wood fire was ignited outside the tent. Once the fire was a clump of coals, a steel grill went over the coals and we plopped our aluminum foil-wrapped dinners on the grill.

After dinner we talked about sled racing dogs, particularly at Iditarod. I asked Tasha, "Are Iditarod mushers still disqualified if a dog dies on the trail?"

She said, "No."

One of the other guests asked, with a little alarm, "You mean dogs actually die running?"

Tasha said dogs do die. She noted as well that dogs die in the kennels. The dogs really want to run. It's what they do. Tasha also said, "Marathon runners sometimes die."

As a one-time marathon runner, I jumped back in the conversation. Sure, it's tough. But I'd trade the quality of life of a back-of-the-pack marathon runner, like me, for the life of the wealthiest couch potato in Los Angeles!

Jack London wrote, "There is an ecstasy that marks the summit of life, and beyond which life cannot rise. And such is the paradox of living, this ecstasy comes when one is most alive, and it comes as a complete forgetfulness that one is alive." (*The Call of the Wild*) Indeed, and the dogs are most alive when they are dragging a sled through the snow, even with a duffer like me behind.

About 9:30, I told folks I was getting cold and going to bed. I crawled in my sleeping bag, pulled a fleece hood over my head, zipped up the sleeping bag, and went to sleep. Folks began to rustle around about 6:00. First task, a reprise of last night, was to feed the dogs.

After our breakfast, we hitched up the dogs. Since Tasha and I were last into camp yesterday, our dogs were the nearest to the trail and we went out first. We rigged the dogs and Tasha led the way.

When we got back to the kennel, we dismantled the teams. I was surprised how attached I was to "my" team. Of course, I know they were fickle – they would love anybody who came to pat and hug them.

On the wall of the lodge was a painting of Ed, leaving Anchorage on his rookie Iditarod. When asked, he explained that since he and his brother were little, they exchanged gag gifts and his brother commissioned an artist to render Ed's first few steps on the Iditarod trail. I said, "That's not a gag gift!" Ed agreed.

Even as a duffer, following sled dogs though the woods was pretty neat.

.

Glen Beatty, our guide, and Craig with a monster pike on the fly rod.

Chapter 18
Armed with 8-weights and Zonker Strips, Craig and Tim Take on the "Frog Thieves"

Craig, my son, and I were admonished – over and over – by Glen Beatty, "Don't throw there; that's a frog thief. Keep it away from the frog thieves."

We had some trouble avoiding the frog thieves. For one thing, Glen's frog thieves were northern pike less than 12 or 15 pounds. And those guys, particularly the smaller ones, were quick as a wink. Dozens of times, as our fly drifted enticingly past a monster pike, a smaller fish darted ahead of the trophy, grabbed the fly and took off. Pretty tough duty, fending off the 5 and 10 pounders on our 8-weight fly rods! For another, much to Glen's chagrin, Craig and I were having a ball catching the frog thieves.

Craig and I were fishing at the prime time for trophy pike – early spring. We arrived at Wolf Bay Lodge on Phelps Lake in northeastern Saskatchewan just after ice out. Indeed, Brent Osika, owner of the lodge, had earlier warned us that the lake might not be open for plane landings. Northern pike spawn in cold water, perhaps under thawing ice, in early spring. They then linger in the spawning bays, soaking up the warmth from spring sunshine. At that time, they are within range of anglers sight-fishing.

My opinion – take it for what it's worth. In more than half a century of pike fishing, there is no method of trophy pike fishing more exciting than sight-fishing with a fly rod. When the monsters are shallow, it's possible for veteran guides like Glen to demand his anglers cast only to trophies.

Craig and I each had our favorite 8-weight fly rods with matching reels and floating lines.

In years past while fly fishing for pike, I had relied on cable leaders to avoid bite-offs. At Glen's suggestion a year earlier, I switched to a length of titanium as the business end of our leaders. Titanium is available in long coils. Craig and I cut off a length of titanium wire, usually 15 inches long, plus or minus. The basic leader should be monofilament, at least 6-feet long and not longer than 9 feet, tapered to 10 pound test. At the monofilament end of the leader, we doubled the titanium into a loop. With an Albright knot, we fastened the monofilament to the titanium. We attached the flies to the titanium with a clinch knot. We pulled the clinch knot tight with pliers. The knot will never reach the "pulled tight" dimensions of a comparable knot of monofilament. But it held. And unlike cable leader tippets, the titanium did not kink. When the titanium piece got too short after changing flies several times, we replaced it.

Glen led us up and down Phelps Lake to shallow bays with names like

Mickey Mouse, Perfection, Reel Good, Frog, Bay of Colossus, Mushroom and Seahorse. All held trophy pike. What did these bays share besides the trophies?

One thing they shared was they were protected from the main portions of the lake. As an upshot, cooler surface water could not be blown into the bays as easily as would have been possible with more open-mouthed bays. Consequently, these bays were warmer than other bays or the open lake. Immediate post-spawn pike spend a few days recovering in relatively warm water.

For another, they were pretty shallow. From the mouth of the bay, all the way to the back, we usually could see the bottom. And often we could see the pike outlined if they were over patches of sand.

Also, the most productive bays were predominantly "black bottom." At times the dark bottom was only in patches, but more commonly the entire substrate was dark. Dark bottoms warm earlier than sand bottoms, thus facilitating eggs to mature more rapidly. For reasons I do not understand, round or nearly-round bays seemed more productive of trophy pike than more angular ones.

Typically, we motored into the chosen bay and began casting as Glen maneuvered the boat along the bank. Usually we were casting about 40 feet. This distance was well within the range of most fly rod anglers, even beginners with a couple of lessons. From time-to-time Glen suggested a cast to a specific spot, but usually Craig and I merely picked our own targets.

In most of the bays we fished, even those of several hundred acres like Seahorse, we soon had big pike located. Then we fished by sight. At times we took turns casting. At others we were both casting to cruising pike. Our casting was facilitated because I cast left-handed and Craig casts right-handed. As a consequence, we were casting with our rods away from one another. Often we agreed, "You cast toward that one and I'll cast to this one." Three times during the week, we each had a 40 inch fish on at the same time.

The secret was to cast within the range of big pike and let the fly settle close to the fish's mouth. Glen provided a running commentary. "Let it sink. She sees it. Strip. Strip. Strip. Stop. She's got it! Set the hook!" Then battle would be on.

Setting the hook with a fly rod was different than with a bait caster (or spinning) gear commonly used by pike anglers. For one thing, a fly rod was much more flexible than a bait casting rod. With a bait casting rod, an effective hook set was usually accomplished by a sharp lifting of the rod tip. With a fly rod lifting the rod tip to set the hook, the flex in the rod absorbed the energy of the lift, never moving the fly in the pike's mouth. During the retrieve, we pointed the rod directly at the fly. Any action to the fly should be imparted by stripping line by hand. When the pike turned and began to pull – not when the white of the pike's mouth was visible over your fly – we stripped hard, two or three times. We set the hook with the line-strip and the butt of the rod. Once the hook set was solid, we lifted the rod.

Fly reels, unlike bait casting or spinning reels, were supplemental in fighting fish. Usually, I managed the battle with a hooked fish by hand. I stripped line, under a finger on the rod above the reel, so I could gain line and let it pay out through my hand when the fish ran. One upshot of that technique was the deck must be clear of pliers, extraneous lures (I'm notorious for switching lures and leaving the discarded one on the deck), or other gear which may be tangled in the stripped line as it falls on the deck. Several times when fishing at Phelps Lake, big pike pulled sufficient line to draw backing off my reel – standard fly line length is 90-feet.

Without losing attention to maintaining tension on the line, we used the reel to play the fish. Most 8-weight matching reels have a drag mechanism, though the drag on a fly reel is rarely as useful as that on a bait caster. If all line was on the reel and the fish runs, we "palmed" the reel spool edge to increase or decrease tension. Truth be told, Craig was much more effective than I in getting the line onto the reel and using the reel to fight the fish.

While it may seem that fly rods were pretty wimpy gear to take on trophy pike quite the reverse is true. Surely, you cannot muscle a 20-pound fish to boat side with a fly rod. Yet, the long rod provided plenty of leverage. Alternate the strength of the rod butt and the flexibility of the tip as demanded by the fish, and pretty big pike can be taken in a relatively modest time. When the fish lunged, we utilized the flexibility of the rod to absorb the shock. During a long run, we put pressure on the fish with the butt. Unless the angler made a mistake, however, even a monster pike ought not to be able to put a direct pull against the strength of the leader. Lots of us have caught fish that exceeded the direct pull strength of the leader.

Pike were taken on a variety of flies. At times, surface flies like a Dahlberg Diver or Peck's Popper worked great. This winter, I'm planning to tie some deer hair mice for next spring's trip. When the big pike were recovering from the spawn, as they were when Craig and I were fighting off the frog thieves, a slowly sinking fly worked best. None better than a fly made of a zonker strip. A zonker strip is a 1/8th inch wide strip of rabbit fur. I tied pike flies on 1/0 or 2/0 hooks with straight eyes. For many fly rod pike anglers, flies tied with zonker strips are called "bunnies." For flies that sank a little faster, I wrapped the shank of the hook with lead before tieing the zonker strips. The best colors were all black, black- and- orange, red-and-white – these are typical "best" colors for pike.

Last winter I tied up a number of minnow-style flies with epoxy heads and made of artificial fibers that worked great for the pike we caught at Phelps Lake. Brown or black back and white belly were particularly effective. With a mixture of black-and-green on the back, white on the bottom, and marked with slanted black lines with a water-proof marker provides a great perch pattern.

I began my long career pike fishing in northern Michigan, and I still spend part of each summer there. Trophy pike there, in contrast to Phelps Lake, are rare. In the small lake near our cabin, the pike are usually below 5 pounds. For these fish, a fly rod is an ideal approach. I often take my fly rod and tube boat to the lake and spend the day catching and releasing these pike.

And why did Glen call them "frog thieves"? Glen carries a bait caster rigged with a hookless rubber frog. In the event his clients seem unable to lure a pike into striking, Glen throws the rubber frog to attract a pike within range. Non-trophy pike often grab the frog and run off with it, and because the frog has no hook, Glen can't prevent them from stealing his frog. So, don't throw to the frog thieves.

Here I am with a pike much bigger than the frog thieves Glen worried about.

Chapter 19
Fishing with Nancy

Nancy knew, before we were married in July, 1965, I was interested in fishing. That knowledge inspired her father, Herbert Krumpeck, to put a dozen brown trout in the irrigation pond at his nursery. Krump, as Nancy's mother and I called him, owned Michigreen Nursery in Grand Haven, Michigan. He had Christmas tree plantations scattered across western Michigan. Krump told me before the wedding he wanted to eat the trout and it was up to me to get them out of the pond.

The pond was 70 or 80 feet long, 20 feet wide and a dozen feet deep. It was fed by cold water seeps and rarely used for irrigation. Easy pickins,' I thought. Wrong.

I started with dry flies, casting from the bank. After all, these were pretty dumb trout accustomed to munching anything that fell in the water. But they did not want dry flies like Adams or Royal Coachman. Though there were grasshoppers along the banks, the trout did not want Dave's Hopper. Wet flies and streamers came to a similar ignominious end.

Nightcrawlers. I was reduced to catching trout with nightcrawlers. I had to lie on my belly on the bank and toss the crawlers gently into the pond. In high school I made a long, slender float of white cedar for perch fishing with minnows. It had a hole in one end to string the line. With a rubber band I could adjust the bobber so it would lay flat on the water or stand upright signaling what kind of bite I had. Flat worked for picky biters, and that's what I had to do to provide Krump's dinner.

Who says, they're in the water and can't get out – they'll be easy to catch?

In the 50 plus years we were married, however, Nancy never caught the angling bug. But I tried.

Nancy fishing at Q Creek.

Wyoming – Q Creek Land and Cattle Company

In 1999 I attended the Outdoor Writers Association of America conference in Sioux Falls, South Dakota. During the opening evening of the conference there was a large room in the Conference Center filled with hawkers of wares of interest to outdoor writers. I wandered around, chatting with old friends and making new. At one of the vendor spots an attractive young woman (does anyone know why attractive young women are assigned such tasks?) told me if I put my business card in her fishbowl, I would win a trip for two to Wyoming trout fishing. She already had a couple of hundred cards, but she knew I would win. So, to be accommodating, I tossed my card in with the others.

An hour or so later during dinner, Cliff Shelby, the conference organizer, announced from the platform, "Tim Mead is the winner of the trout fishing trip to Q Creek Land and Cattle Company in Wyoming ." And

Cliff told me how to redeem the trip.

I was sure Nancy would not want to go and had in my mind I would ask Jeff Samsel, a fellow outdoor writer and longtime friend, go with me. A couple of hours later, however, when I called home to check in and told Nancy I won a trip for two to Wyoming trout fishing, she said, "I'd love to go. That's great."

Q Creek Land and Cattle is a cattle ranch of 560,000 acres, touted as the largest contiguous ranch in Wyoming. Right after World War II the owner was concerned cattle did not have a continuous source of water and dammed small streams throughout the ranch. Later, the resultant ponds were stocked with trout, browns in some, rainbows in some, cutthroats in others. The trout flourished.

In the early 1990s, Q Creek Land and Cattle realized folks would pay big bucks to come fish for these trout. To write articles about the trout fishing – well, that's where Outdoor Writers Association of America and fishbowls full of business cards come in – Q Creek wanted a writer to come, write a story for one of the fishing magazines, and encourage business.

When Nancy and I went, the flight from Charlotte to Chicago was a little late. We had to hustle to catch the flight to Salt Lake. In turn, that flight was a bit tardy, so we did not have time to grab a bite to eat before the flight left for Caspar. The flight to Caspar was also delayed so we would have had time to eat had someone told us. It was late when we got to Casper, about 10:00 local time and midnight back home.

Yet Steve Steinle from Q Creek was there to greet us, grab bags and head to the ranch. A few miles into the ride, he asked, "Did you folks get something to eat?" We said we had not eaten but we would be fine. Then something happened I had never seen before. He made a phone call from the truck. When someone answered, he said, "Our guests have not had anything to eat. We'll be there in an hour. Be sure something is ready."

Ready? At 11:30 we were served a five star dinner, steak and all the trimmings. Truth is, that's how we ate the entire time at Q Creek. Five star.

We had a guide apiece. Nancy's guide was Adrian Keeler from Battle

Creek, Michigan. In conversation, we learned he and I grew up at different times but not far apart. In fact, he said he knew there were Keelers in Springport, Michigan, my home town. "Oh," I said, "Chuck Keeler. He was one of my dad's high school students. He repaired cars in a small garage east of town. When I was in high school, the garage caught fire, and we could see the smoke on the west end of town during baseball practice. I've gotten my oil changed many times at Chuck's garage."

While I had given Nancy fly casting lessons in preparation for the trip, she was more enthusiastic than proficient. She persuaded Adrian the idea of the trip was for her to catch fish and she was more likely to do so if he did the casting. It took some effort, but he was finally convinced. She did catch trout, some nice ones. I fished from my tube boat and as I paddled around the ponds I could hear, "Set, Nancy, set."

Most afternoons, Nancy took off. She rested in the truck used to ferry us about, read, or one day the guide took her back to the lodge.

Once we were home, we invited several couples to dinner to tout the trip to Wyoming. For some years I had been mounting photos of big fish with a consistent pattern of mat and framing. After dinner was over, I showed slides of the trip and presented Nancy with a framed picture matching photos my trophy fish of one of the trout she caught. She hung the framed photo in her office at Mercy Hospital where she was Director of Volunteer Services.

I wrote an article about the trip published in *American Angler*. Another article appeared in *Fur-Fish-Game* and a "Trip Tip" was in *In-Fisherman*.

Montana – Five Rivers Lodge

For several years the traveling Fly Fishing Show came to Charlotte. I always went.

The year after the Wyoming trip as I wandered past booths touting various resorts catering to fly rod anglers, I met Jay Burgin from Five Rivers Lodge in Dillon, Montana. He had seen the article in *American Angler* and offered a comped trip to Five Rivers Lodge. I told him on the trip to Wyoming, my wife also went. He said, "Oh, I'll comp her, too."

We negotiated a time in September of 2000. Among the lessons, for me at least, of the trip to Wyoming was that it was a long way to go to fish a few days and come home. I persuaded Bill Shumaker, both of us newly retired from the faculty at The University of North Carolina at Charlotte, to travel to Montana with me, fish a while, and fly back to Charlotte. In turn, Nancy would fly to Butte, fish for a few days, and fly back to Charlotte. And I would drive home alone.

Five Rivers Lodge is top drawer. The chef had been the main man at a casino in Las Vegas. He travelled on vacation to Montana, liked it so much, he called his employer and quit. He needed a job and signed on at Five Rivers. Meals were out of this world. Each evening at dessert time, Mary, co-owner of Five Rivers, came through, with Montana lottery tickets. She up-fronted all the guests with a modest ticket. If you won, she came back and urged you to double down. We all did, until we all lost everything to the Montana lottery.

Leon Sagaloff was our guide. Over the years I have hired Leon often. We met at Five Rivers, but have become good friends in the intervening years. Leon and Nancy became buddies on the trip. She rode with Leon, wherever we were going to fish, while I drove my truck. Mid-day, Nancy used my truck to return to the lodge.

For Nancy, it was a tough trip. Leon and I got too caught up in the trout fishing. For example, on the Big Hole River, though neither of us noticed, we left Nancy stranded on a rock in mid-stream with no one to help her take the next step. We got her there but then abandoned her.

Furthermore, Nancy did not catch many trout. Despite the casting lessons at Reedy Creek Park, Nancy could not lay out 40 feet of line and leader consistently. Leon and I both began to understand her frustration with fishing and with us and tried to do better. To little avail. The last day we were at the Lodge, I took her down to the ponds on the property and with me casting she caught a couple of nice rainbows.

From the Lodge we went to Yellowstone National Park. We saw Old Faithful and stayed at the Lodge there. Where cars were parked along the road, we stopped and saw a massive bull elk protecting his harem, fending off a young tough with bellows and horn clashes. We wandered from the

West Yellowstone entrance and left the north entrance and headed toward Bozeman.

We made a successful trip of it. But not because of the trout Nancy caught.

Alaska – Bear Trail Lodge

For years I coveted trout fishing in Alaska. As a kid I read Russell Annabell's tales. I understood the implication in Doug Persico's observation when Bill Shumaker and I stayed at Rock Creek Mercantile near Clinton, Montana that trout fishing in Montana was "the best in the lower 48."

I proposed to take son Craig and his wife and Nancy to Alaska, trout fishing. Craig and Nancy said they would go. Scott Swanson, a friend, op-

Nancy with a silver salmon. How her jacket and fingernail polish matched did not show when The Charlotte Observer ran this picture.

erated a fishing oriented travel agency. I contacted Scott and he arranged for us to stay at Bear Trail Lodge near King Salmon.

Nancy did not want to fish every day, so we planned for her to take fly out trips to glaciers and bear watching. I don't think she had ever flown in a plane as small as the bush planes and she enjoyed it.

Caleb Hitzfield, our guide, made an effort to see that Nancy caught fish. The fishing highlight of the trip for Nancy was on the King Salmon River, just a few hundred yards upstream from the Lodge. Silver salmon were in the stream and there were lots of them. The stream was 60 or 70 feet wide and only a few feet deep. The salmon were easy to see. Caleb got us positioned along the river, Craig upstream, me downstream and Nancy in the middle with Caleb coaching. Nancy was using spinning gear and casting a small spinner across the current and reeling it slowly past the salmon.

One grabbed Nancy's lure and headed for Bristol Bay. Line peeled off the reel and Nancy stood transfixed, frozen. Craig and I both put up our gear and soon Nancy had three coaches. It's a wonder she was able to filter out what she needed to do. Nancy was not stable enough in waders and not experienced enough to follow the fish downstream. Without really knowing what would happen but trying to reassure her, I said, "He'll have to come back to you. Just keep the rod tip up and the line tight. Don't jerk."

Sure enough, the salmon began swimming upstream. Nancy reeled frantically trying to keep tension on the line. The fish passed us and Caleb went into the middle of the river with his net. His presence would deter another downstream run where the fish would have his strength and the current working for him.

The fish tired and Caleb netted it. Victory. Caleb lifted the salmon, gave it a whack and held it up for all to see. Nancy asked plaintively, "Aren't I going to be able to hold it?" What Nancy liked most about the picture we took of her holding the fish was her nail polish and jacket matched.

When we got back to Charlotte, I contacted Jack Horan. Jack is a friend and the outdoor guy at *The Charlotte Observer*. I told Jack about Nancy's salmon and that I had a good picture. Jack told me to send the picture and he'd put it in Thursday's sport section. I did not say anything to Nancy, knowing she would not see the picture before she left for Mercy Hospital. When she got to the hospital, folks asked if she had a good trip to Alaska, how she cooked salmon, did she see any bears. Finally, about 10:00 someone asked, "Did you really catch that salmon?" Of course, in the newspaper, no one noticed the color match she thought so crucial.

Condominium – Palencia, Belize

Over time I read about the wonders of bonefish and how delicately they took a fly and how they sped off across the flats. I wanted to give them a try. Because I was taking French at the University, I needed to go on spring break. Scott Swanson, the chap who owned the fishing travel agency and arranged the trip to Alaska, found a condominium in Palencia, Belize we could rent for the crucial week.

The plane from Belize City landed on a single strip of asphalt hacked out of the mangroves. What they did with a cross wind was not clear to me. The "terminal" was a house trailer parked along the asphalt.

The condo was really nice. No restaurant was associated with the units but we discovered after a day or two orders could be phoned in to somewhere and dinner would arrive in half an hour or so. In the evenings, we sat on the porch, ate dinner and watched the Gulf of Mexico.

Victor was our guide. On our first morning, he loaded us on his boat and headed for the barrier reefs, miles into the Gulf. Nancy told me later she was worried we would be lost when all we could see in any direction was water.

Our first stop was at a small, unoccupied island where Victor collected hermit crabs for Nancy to use as bait. At the next stop, we could see schools of bonefish cruising shallow water. Using light spinning gear, Nancy cast one of the crabs as Victor instructed. Sure enough, she caught a couple of bonefish. Then she said she had enough. Victor knew a safe place where she could sit and read for the afternoon. And that was Nancy's fishing trip to Belize.

She took a couple of day trips arranged in advance, one to a set of

Mayan ruins which she enjoyed. On our last day in Belize, we took a guided trip through a jungle nature preserve.

Coda

Nancy never caught it, the addiction to fishing. Fishing for her was like golf or bridge for me.

In late 2015 Nancy was diagnosed with ALS, Lou Gehrig's Disease. She struggled valiantly, but succumbed in February 2016. In the 50 plus years we were married, Nancy never said I spent too much time or money fishing. When I started taking Craig with me, she never complained of being left out. After I dug up the rain-soaked back yard with the 4-wheel drive trying to back the boat into the garage, she did suggest the boat have a tarp and be left in the driveway.

I now seek the new normal. While my lifelong addiction has been fishing. Nancy had hers and fishing was not among them, yet some of our best times were those when she came along for fishing excursions.

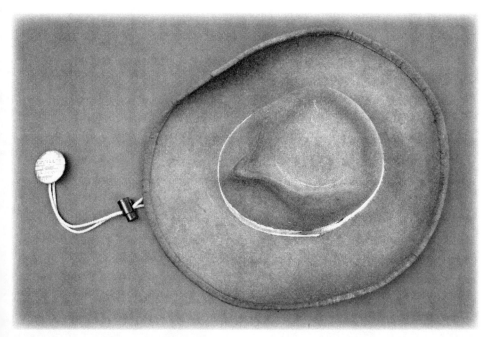

The hat that started the trash talk.

Chapter 20
Talking Trash

Glenn Burne, long-time buddy, took a look at my hat and exclaimed, "My gosh, Bill. I should have worn my hat. Look at Tim's hat. I'm disgraced!"

Glenn, Bill, Larry and I were getting together to plan a fishing and camping trip.

My hat was a felt job purchased nearly 40 years ago at a safari outfitter in Johannesburg, South Africa. Since then it has weathered winter fishing for smallmouth bass, walleyes and muskies in central Pennsylvania, pike and walleye fishing in Ontario, trout fishing in Michigan, Montana, Wyoming, North Carolina and Alaska, largemouth bass fishing in varied locales and the indignities of multiple shots of insect repellent. It has a band of Impala hide and a 1975 Pennsylvania fishing license soldered to the lanyard. It's a delightful mess. Often someone admires my hat, some in genuine envy, some in mock admiration.

Glenn, to his dismay, was wearing a simple baseball cap with the name of some plastic worm on it. His hat was clearly outclassed by mine. Yet, he claimed, he could have worn his New Zeeland Clancy style angler's hat, Clancy apparently the generic name for a sheepherder. Glenn recounted he had worn the hat trout fishing in the Arizona and Colorado mountains. He said it weathered rain storms and insect infestations. But thinking he needed to make a good impression at the planning session, he left it home.

As a result of the exchange between Glenn and me, all had to listen as I told them the origin of my hat and the places it had been in the interim. After all, that's the function of "talking trash," to give someone a short term advantage. From the distant upper seats of arenas across the country, we see the home team and their opponents "talking trash." Among outdoor folk, talking trash serves the same function.

Many years ago, while fishing with Craig, then my five or six year old son, I caught a nice two pound plus largemouth bass. Craig, however, caught two, albeit smaller ones. He insisted we take them home to show his mother. For several weeks he regaled all within earshot. And I heard back, "I hear Craig outfished you two-to-one." I never got a chance to explain my fish was bigger or it was my knowledge which put us where the fish were or I told Craig where to cast. People I did not know approached me and asked, "Are you the guy whose kid outfished him the other evening?" Craig's trash talking gave him the edge.

Sometimes Craig's trash talking has worked to my advantage. On a family vacation to Kitty Hawk, North Carolina, on a bright summer day, most anglers up-and-down the beach had given up. Yet, I located a spot 70 or 80 feet off the bank and there were fish in it. I had seven or eight in my bucket. A chap appeared next to me. He asked, pointing to Craig playing in the sand, "Is that your son?" he asked, "he just told you were the best fisherman on the beach and I should look in your bucket. I don't know what kind of fish those are, but they should make a nice family dinner."

Dick Jones was among the best trash talkers I ever knew. When I was a teenager in Springport, Michigan, Dick, though an adult, was one of my fishing buddies. He lugged me all over the state.

Dick and Dad had a running trash talking which ran a couple of years. Since I was not present, I cannot attest to either side of the dialogue. Dick and Dad, along with Dick's father, went to Long Lake in the Upper Peninsula (I know, there are many Long Lakes and there are some long lakes). They rented a round bottom boat and portaged it to the lake. While miles from shore, high wind and rain drove them to seek shelter on shore.

Hours later, they returned to the landing and what happened next depends on whose trash you believe. Dick's dad got out of the boat and took an armload of gear toward the car. According to Dick, my dad then picked up the several anchors they had, stood near the edge of the boat, and threw himself into the chilly lake. "You should have seen him," Dick chortled. "He grabbed those anchors, some in each hand, and dove into the lake."

"Dick, the boat would not have tipped if you hadn't pulled the bow onto the log. Everybody who knows anything knows you cannot pull a round bottom boat onto a log. The boat will tip every time. You pitched me into the water. I didn't fall."

Each time they repeated this tale, the wind and rain grew stronger, the roundness of the boat and the slipperiness of the log increased. The laughter of listeners and the friendship of the trash talkers increased.

Different perhaps than the trash talking of professional athletes, but a key component of friendship among outdoor enthusiasts is the trash talking that goes on. It's verbal "one upmanship." Each year for the last 20, Gordy Johnson, Tony Garitta, Clyde Osborne and I made a trek into one lodge or another in Ontario. It will be this year, as it has been every year in the past, constant trash talk. We will be stronger because of it.

Chapter 21
Golden Opportunity

From the time I was high school dreaming, perhaps lusting, after exotic fishing destinations, among them were backcountry alpine lakes. Gorgeous scenery. Dumb trout. Wilderness. What could be better?

When I learned the Outdoor Writers Association of America (OWAA) would meet in Billings, Montana, I anticipated an opportunity to hike to and camp at an alpine lake and fish for trout. Despite trips all over Montana exploring trout venues, I had never been to one of the high country lakes. Jack Ballard, fellow outdoor writer and a friend, was the local conference coordinator. He was sure to know a suitable spot for such an adventure. I contacted Jack and asked for a suggestion.

He responded he was going to organize such a trip after the conference and I was welcome to join it. Jack proposed a hike of five and a half miles into Sylvan Lake, Montana's premier spot for golden trout. The trail would be over a ridge, a change in elevation of roughly 3000 feet. On a layover day, Jack planned to hike another couple of miles, maybe a little more, to Crow Lake for brook trout. I signed up.

After the conference, we rendezvoused at the home of Jack and Lisa Ballard in Red Lodge. Lisa had just finished a term as President of OWAA. Some of those over-nighting at Ballard's were not making the trip to Sylvan Lake.

After breakfast, Jack rounded up those headed for the high country. We wandered about, ever higher. We made the trailhead near East Rosebud Lake. Elevation, about 6000 feet. The highest point in North Carolina, Mt. Mitchell is 6,684 feet. The highest I had hiked in the Tar Heel State was to Cold Mountain, 6032 feet (see Chapter 12, "Journey to Cold Mountain"). At home, the elevation is 734 feet. At the trailhead, I was already in high country.

We set off. Gradually Jim Low, Birdie Hawkins and I were bringing up the rear. After a couple of miles, Birdie went ahead, leaving Jim and me. The higher we got, the slower I went. Breathing became ever harder. Not gasping, really, but I simply could not get enough oxygen each breath to support the exertion. I urged Jim to leave me, but he insisted he was slowing down, too. On we went, stopping periodically to catch our breath, peering at the valley we left behind, speculating how far we had come and how far we had to go.

At roughly 2:00, Jack appeared on the trail ahead of us. "Whose pack should I take first?" he asked. Before either Jim or I could answer, Jack said, "Tim, give me your pack." I insisted I could make it, and Jack responded, "I know you can, but I'll carry it for a while." I recalled on trips to Quetico Park when I was taking novice voyageurs, I insisted we would make community decisions but if it comes to a matter of safety, "I decide." Jack was the leader (he said "scoutmaster") of this trip, had lots more experience in high country than I, and, in effect, he was telling me it was a matter of safety and he was deciding. I gave him my pack.

Perhaps half a mile further, Jack said, "This is a shortcut," and headed up a 45° slope. The trail, not apparent on the rocky substrate, was marked periodically by small rock cairns, what folks in the canoe country of Minnesota and Ontario call Inusuks. Every couple of hundred yards, Jack paused for a minute or two while Jim and I caught our breath. No doubt about it, oxygen was pretty scarce. Half a mile from meeting Jim and me, Jack said, "This is the peak. It's downhill from here to camp."

Shortly after 3:00 we broke into a clearing. Jack asked where I wanted my pack, and I said, "Right here." And that's where I pitched my tent.

All the other anglers were already at the lake, perhaps a quarter mile from camp, fishing. Jim and I established our sites as quickly as we could, strung up our rods and headed for the lake. I was sufficiently oxygen deprived I found the short trip, over a small ridge, "breath taking."

I began fishing with a #14 Purple Haze and almost immediately began to catch golden trout. None were trophies, but solid 10 or 12 inch fish. And stunningly beautiful. Are golden trout the most beautiful trout? Hard

Here I am, catching a golden trout at Sylvan Lake.

for me to say. Who ever saw an ugly trout? I had heard golden trout did not give a very good account of themselves on the business end of a fly line. Yet, they seemed plenty strong to me, comparable to other trout of the same size.

Bill Powell and Chris Madson had ten trout strung on a stick. Jim and I added one each, so we had an even dozen to share at dinner. Roasted in the coals, the fresh trout were a suitable end to a lovely day.

I told Jack I was not going to make the trip into Crow Lake the next day. I would stay at Sylvan Lake and rest for the hike out in two days. He said that was fine and probably a good idea.

I crawled in my tent a little after 8:00 and went to sleep, no tossing or turning. Just sleep.

In the morning, I grabbed my fly rod out of the Loblolly Pine where I stashed it the evening before and headed for the lake. I tied a small beetle pattern on the end of my leader. Somewhere I read a major forage in the relatively sterile alpine lakes were terrestrials of one sort or another. Besides, I lost my Purple Haze in the bushes on an errant backcast last evening. Bill and Chris were already fishing and Jim came to the lake about when I did.

Casting from the spot where I first hit the lake, one of my first casts drew a taker. Turns out it was the consensus largest trout of the trip, a beautiful fish, measured by hand at 16 inches, plus or minus. Before breakfast, I caught three.

After breakfast, Jack, Bill, Chris and Jim headed for Crow Lake. I went back to Sylvan Lake to catch golden trout. Most of the time, there was a little breeze. Fishing with dry flies, each of us simply cast. Let the fly drift with the wind. That's what anything natural would do. Trout in lakes or ponds are not taking a position oriented to the current and waiting for a morsel to be brought to them. These trout cruise, looking, looking, looking. In a couple of hours, I caught five more, all about the same size we had been catching.

After lunch, I took a nap.

About 3:00, I headed back to the lake. Where the trail met the lake, a long point extended to the right. I crossed the point to fish someplace I had not tried. Once there, the floor of the lake was rock-strewn with water I guessed four or five feet deep at the most. The breeze was coming around the point, left to right. I began to cast 35 or 40 feet and gradually extended the distance of my casts, a foot or so at a time, out to 50 feet or so. Each cast I allowed my fly to drift until I could tell the line developed a bow which would prevent me from hooking a fish were it to take the fly. Then I took a few steps to the right and repeated the process. As was true the entire time we fished Sylvan Lake, frequently a trout took something on or near the surface. Since these were cruising, casting to a rise made little sense. Unlike trout in a stream, any fish we saw move would be moving on. Yet, the surface activity always raised our hopes and assured us trout were active. In the afternoon, I caught another five golden trout.

All-in-all, I caught enough golden trout to be able to answer, "Have you ever caught golden trout?" with "Several." I cannot answer, "Many."

At dinner, I told Jack I wanted to start down to the trailhead in the morning ahead of the rest of the crew. Jim said he would go with me as we both felt we needed a head start. Jack said I should leave part of my gear and he, Bill and Chris would divvy it and carry it out. While I protested, I appreciated Jack's proposition. In the morning he told me to leave my tent, sleeping bag and pad. At breakfast, Jack claimed my stove and its fuel.

As I got ready to leave, I started along the path, the long way round. Jack said I should take the short cut over the ridge. I told him I was not confident of my ability to follow the rocky trail, unmarked by mashed down grass as is the case with forest trails I know. Bill Powell grabbed his pack and said he would lead Jim and me. Off we went, back up the incline we had come down two days before.

Golden trout on display. Some thought this 16 inch fish was the largest of the trip and I may as well go along.

Once we crossed the ridge and started down, it seemed to me each step made it easier to breathe. It was still tough, have no doubt. We stopped at a small creek, perhaps one quarter of the way back to the trailhead for Bill to change from long pants into shorts. From time-to-time Bill slowed or stopped. We chatted about our experiences on other trips, folks we knew in common, folks only one of us knew. We came across a spot near the trail where a northern flicker had met his demise. Once we were well down the trail, perhaps three quarters of the distance needed, Bill said if it was OK with us, he would trek on ahead. Jim and I agreed and off he went.

Later, the rest of our companions passed us. Birdie and Hannah lingered on the trail, still behind us. Jim speculated they were extending us a courtesy lest we be passed by girls. Sometimes they were close behind and we could hear them talking, sometimes farther and we could not.

At 78 years old, I was the geezer by 20 years. Though I try not to think in terms of "bucket lists," I probably waited too long to make a trek to an alpine lake. For years I have been what some think of as a fitness nut. Most days I work out at a local gym. In preparation for the trip, I added a stair climber to my routine, and I cranked up the resistance. But I was unable to prepare for the thin air. Yet, I had a wonderful time, though I shall not make such a hike again. I'll stick to lower climes.

A triple golden opportunity. Golden trout, good friends, and the trip of a lifetime. Can't get much better than that.

Chapter 22
Sutton River Brook Trout

My huge, size 8, Turck's Tarantula bobbed along the current, just beyond a dense weed bed. A few moments earlier Len Anderson, my canoe partner, suggested, "If you have something that will float and not get tangled in those weeds, this would be a good place to start."

We had just begun a ten day float trip from Haley Lake in northern Ontario, down the Sutton River (going north on the map, so it may not seem like "down" to some) 85 miles to Hudson Bay. Part of the trip would be through Polar Bear Provincial Park. There were eight of us in four canoes, all loaded with camping and fishing gear – no motels or lodges on this trip.

My fly floated a dozen feet or so when a 17 inch brook trout appeared below it and sucked it under. Maybe not the first cast of the trip, but one of the first. To the amusement of Len and the pair in the canoe behind us, Lloyd Hautajarvi and Randy Hicks, I said, "That's the biggest brook trout I ever hooked. That's the biggest brook trout I ever saw."

Len assured me, "It won't be the biggest by quite a bit." He was more insightful than I could imagine. We only fished half a day as we flew from Hearst, Ontario to Hawley Lake buffeted by high winds. By the end of the day Len's prediction was vindicated.

I wasn't the only one catching trophy brook trout. As we set up camp and ate dinner, exultations abounded. Save Len and Stu Osthoff, both of whom visited the Sutton River before, we all claimed to have caught "the biggest brook trout ever." We could scarcely comprehend each would catch more, larger ones in the days ahead.

Breaking camp each morning, including a hot breakfast, kept us from the water early. Most days we started fishing about 9:30 or 10:00. For-

Sutton River brook trout.

tunately for the early risers, Len made plenty of coffee and conversation ranged widely over places we fished in the past and hoped to fish in the future.

The first two and a half days fishing was devoted to locating trout near weed beds. Weeds waved in the current and trout were in them. On the first day, a large, pale mayfly hatched sporadically. Water never boiled with feeding trout, but there were lots of rising fish and they loved the Turck's Tarantula. Len maneuvered the canoe to maximize my opportunities. At times we simply drifted and each of us caught fish.

Among the brookies I caught was one which showed between weeds and a grassy, undercut, bank. Len and I both saw the fish rise ahead of the canoe. With Len's encouragement, I cast to the lane which would carry my fly over the fish. As it neared the spot, I said, "If he's going to take it should be just about now." On cue, an 18 inch trout took my fly.

All day long, Len and I drifted slowly, casting to pockets in the swirling weeds. Brook trout I scarcely imagined as a youth in Michigan came to our flies. Although I offered Len a Turck's Tarantula, he fished with a Muddler Minnow and it worked as well as my fly. Since Len periodically guided the canoe, he made fewer casts than I. Action was steady all day. Between us, we caught over 50 brook trout a little above or below 20 inches.

The next day was a mirror image of the day before.

Gradually the Sutton River changed. Weed beds did not disappear, but they became much less common. Whereas the first few days the river changed direction gradually, now it became a typically meandering stream with sharp bends, often switching directions as much as 90 degrees.

Pools at the bends were now prime holding spots for trout. Fishing became more productive and predicable. At one pool where I was wading, Dave Brewer and Tom Spence drifted through and Dave advised me, "The tail of this pool starts right here." I took a few steps downstream, casting a large pink-and-white zonker streamer I tied to go pike fishing. In the 10 minutes I fished the spot Dave suggested, I caught two brook trout which in earlier times I would have marked as all time greats. Now I simply accepted them as nice fish and released them.

In addition to the zonker, I also fished a #8 Matuka streamer. Cast quartering downstream, stripped in six inch to one foot jerks, then allowed to swing directly below me also drew strikes. If they hit on one of the jerks the strikes were jolts.

Clearly, however, in the pools and the runs between the pools, the most productive fly was a deer hair bass bug. When we got together for lunch or in the evening to set up camp, everyone had been catching trout on mice, Dahlberg divers, sliders or some other deer hair pattern.

In my fly box I had eight deer hair bass bugs. All of them finished the trip destroyed – tails ripped off, clumps of hair missing, eyes gone. Eventu-

Sutton River brook trout.

ally I was fishing what was left as a partially buoyant streamer. Randy had a pink monstrosity deer hair popper and it was deadly.

One afternoon I stood at the edge of a pool and caught fish after fish after fish. Stu wanted us to keep a count of the trout we landed and I claimed 61 for the day. I was not top angler. Len fished just upstream from me and around the corner, out of sight. When I looked his way I often saw his bowed rod over the shoreline grass as he too battled brookies. Two of the trout I caught in this pool were just short of 24 inches, the biggest I ever caught (though others on the trip caught larger ones).

After we set up camp that afternoon, I was walking along the bank as Len fished the far side of the stream. I saw a fish move and I yelled to Len, "Big fish just moved between you and the rock where we started to catch fish this morning."

"I can't see the rock from here," he answered. "There's too much glare

169

on the water."

"OK, make another cast in the same direction but about 15 feet further."

Len and I began to get razzing from the others. "What happens if his 15 feet is different from yours?" Ignoring the gallery, Len stripped more line and cast. Perfect.

As his deer hair mouse drifted toward the rock, I yelled at Len, "Ought to be right about there." A nice brook trout rose to the fly. Shoreline hecklers cheered.

Runs between pools also held trout. Particularly as we moved downstream, we began to see more boulders in the River. We really never had pocket water sluicing between multiple large rocks. The boulders, however, concentrated trout in locations comparable to rocks in pocket water. At one of the spots where we stopped for lunch, I was fishing one side of the stream and several were fishing the other. We caught fish, with different flies and somewhat different presentations, from the same spot below the same rocks.

On a cloudy day, as Len and I paddled downstream looking for an ideal spot to drag the canoe ashore and fish, Len asked, "What's that on the bank?"

"Where?" I answered. "I don't see anything."

"Ahead of us." Len said. "Just a few feet from the tree line, looking right at us. In fact, coming toward us."

With Len's instruction, I saw it too. About the size and shape of a domestic dog, brown with white blotches. An artic fox. I was pretty sure of my judgment and confirmed my identification when I got home and consulted my field guides.

Gradually, the river widened and straightened. The brook trout, however, were still there and plentiful. With the same flies, we continued to catch fish. Late one afternoon, all four canoes were dragged on a mid-river shoal. From where I stood, I could see all eight in our group. Len was just upstream from me. As we were both battling a trout, Len said, "Look. Right now six of us have a fish on." He was right. Earlier I noted often Len and I were both tangled with a trout at the same time. Now, however, the group had more than merely a "double." How many times had that happened when the others were out if sight?

Based on their earlier trips, Len and Stu determined fishing slacked off in the last 20 miles. We agreed the last day should be devoted to paddling to the pickup spot a few miles from Hudson Bay.

Stu and Kim Lulloff, in the lead, suddenly pulled their canoe onto the bank. Stu yelled, "Everybody on the bank."

Those of us in the trailing canoes asked one another, "What's going on?"

Then we saw a small polar bear splash across the river, scramble up the far bank and run into the sparse trees. Stu was concerned that a frightened polar bear was not to be taken lightly and moved us aside.

A couple of miles later, a barren ground caribou thundered along the right bank and ran at least half a mile before heading into the shrubbery.

Mid-afternoon, Stu led the canoes to the bank where a small stream entered the main flow. "OK," he said, "here's a good place for everyone to catch one more fish." We grabbed our rods and within moments each of us caught "one last fish," some of us several times. These brook trout were as stout and eager to take our flies as any other on the trip.

The closer we got to Hudson Bay, the cloudier the weather. From time-to-time, we paddled through a heavy mist. A few miles from the last camp site and the spot where we would be picked up by a float plane, on the left bank we saw a huge polar bear. Rather than paddle a few yards from the bear, Stu had us beach the canoes on an island a hundred yards from the squatting critter. Even at that distance, the bear looked pretty big. Lots bigger than any I ever saw at a zoo. Was he sizing us up to determine which was the slowest runner?

We paddled around, avoiding a direct presentation to the bear. When we got around the island where we might see him again, he was gone.

While I did not maintain a precise count, I believe on the trip I caught 200 brook trout 20 inches or more. Monster brook trout haunted my dreams as a boy. No more haunts now.

Geezers ought to be able to catch nice trout, like this brookie, in comfort and safety.

Chapter 23
Geezer Trout

Genetics seems to be the solution to everything these days. Back when I went to high school biology no one had ever heard of genes. Now, manipulate the genes of some plant or animal and get disease-resistant corn or fat-free beef. It's progress, no matter how you look at it.

As trout anglers age, some of their needs change. While it is too late to modify the genes of some of my angling buddies (or me), now just might be the time to begin developing a strain of trout, a genetic manipulation we might call "geezer preference." These trout would have the genetic qualities to assure my friends could catch trout like they used to (or remember they used to).

For one thing, geezer preference trout would not strike at flies smaller than, say, size 14. Even with a parachute dry fly tied with a fluorescent post, a number 20 blue wing olive drifting down a stream on a typical blue wing olive day is virtually invisible. Sometimes the only indication a trout has taken a fly is a tug on the line. How many strikes are missed? No one knows.

Further, tiny flies are ever more difficult to tie on tiny tippets. The next time I see Dr. Sie, my eye doctor, I'm going to show her a number 20 gold-ribbed hare's ear and a 7X tippet and tell her, "I want be able to thread this line through the eye on this hook."

Fishing in Montana a while back, I noticed Bill, a long-time buddy, kept going back to the lodge. When I asked him why he returned so often he told me he wanted the 20 year old waitress to tie on a new fly for him.

Geezer preference trout would like gaudy flies. A friend suggested green drakes would be suitable. I told him what I had in mind was more like an orange drake.

And geezer preference trout would strike deliberately. So often a rainbow appears from nowhere, slashes at a drifting fly, and disappears before a geriatric angler can respond. In addition to the difficulty in hooking such rapidly striking trout, there is danger to anglers as well. Dale, one of my angling pals, tumbled backward into a stream trying to set the hook on a trout in the North Carolina mountains.

Bass anglers claim if a largemouth bass grabs a Texas-rigged plastic worm and holds on for three seconds the typical fisherperson can successfully set the hook. Given the limitations of folks who fish for bass compared to those who seek trout, trout anglers would not need so much time. Geezer preference trout should be genetically engineered to grasp a fly and hold on for 2.5 seconds, with a standard deviation not to exceed .5.

With more and more anglers practicing catch-and-release and more states adopting delayed harvest to spread the availability of trout fishing, except for deep wilderness fish, trout seem to be getting smarter every day. The day of "dumb" trout just dropped off the hatchery truck has passed me by. Geezer preference trout would have short memories. Simply because a 14 inch brown trout got caught on Tuesday on a size 10 Adams would not mean the same fly would not work on Wednesday. Maybe trout studies could be tied to Alzheimer's disease research in humans – diminished memory in one and enhanced memory in the other.

While we still want trout to lie in current breaks, spots ancient anglers have learned over the years, geezer preference trout would seek substrates where the rocks were not covered with slick algae. The Big Hole River and Rock Creek, both in southwestern Montana, are beautiful streams teeming with trout. Like many other streams across the country, wading these streams is a constant struggle. For me, the struggle has become more intense as each year passes. From direct experience, I can attest the water is cold. An early morning dip in a trout creek can ruin a day's fishing.

Geezer preference trout would be genetically encouraged to prefer streams with a modest gradient. What would be appropriate? Certainly any stream where water is clearly running downhill, swirling around rocks and into deep holes is too swift. Stream trout are toughened by current, no doubt. Yet, there ought to be a limit.

A couple of months ago, Bob Martin alerted me to another danger of swift water. Bob is not yet a geezer, but he's approaching it. We were fishing the Stillwater River in Montana. The Stillwater is not still water. It was eager to get wherever it was going. The bottom was covered with slick, basketball size rocks. When we met for lunch, Bob told me he lost the studs off his boots. "No way," I told him, "those things are screwed in tight." I was wrong. Bob did lose the studs off both boots. If that happened to a geezer, it could be a real threat.

Of course, a careful angler can, and should, get a wading staff. Bill bought a shock-corded collapsible pole at a yard sale. He used it as an aid to wading. It was completely white. I accused Bill of trying to fool trout into thinking he was blind and they could strike his fly with impunity. He merely wanted to take advantage of me. He denied, of course, the merit of my analysis.

Geezer preference trout would not be leader shy. When a couple of extra false casts are required to dry a favorite fly, perhaps even after the fly caught a fish, trout would not head for the nearest log jam or under-cut bank. How many times has the first hint I had trout were around was when I noted a flash as the fish headed for cover?

In order to protect genetically specialized trout, sections of streams would need to be set aside for senior anglers. Sort of like catch-and-re-lease, flies only, delayed harvest and other restricted areas. From time-to-time, of course, trout from other sections would infiltrate the geezer portions. Consequently, there would always be the possibility a savvy, leader shy, midge sipper might appear. Such fish would merely add to the challenge.

An alternative to geezer preference trout, I guess, would be more TV shows about trout fishing. We could sit home and watch younger folks catch fish. I'd rather do the catching myself.

Chapter 24
Seeing Is Believing:
Rainbows on the Bighorn

Jon Madsen and I waded, ankle-deep, beside a long braid. Jon peered intently into the rushing water. Suddenly he said, "There's one. Right there. And that's a feeding trout. He just moved and took something."

To myself I thought, "I don't care if this guy is supposed to be the best guide on the Bighorn. He can't see a feeding trout there." We were adjacent to a 200 yard riffle. Water tumbled over basketball-sized rocks and between strands of waving reeds. The surface was broken and glistening in the bright sunlight. Clearly, Jon was putting me on.

But he insisted. "Between the weeds, the water is 18 inches to two feet deep," he said. That part I could believe.

"There, that fish just moved again. You're going to catch that fish," Jon assured me.

When we began the day, just below the Yellowtail Dam near Fort Smith, Montana, Jon rigged Bill Shumaker and me with a classic double nymph and strike indicator. Shortly after launching the boat, Jon pulled it up on a rocky shoreline. He stationed Bill at the head of a run, coached him a little, and led me to the riffle.

Jon told me how much line to pull off my reel and the precise angle to begin casting. "About quartering upstream, toward that cottonwood on the far bank," he said. Since I was paying for the advice, I did just as he suggested. After I made a couple of casts Jon said, "Your flies are passing just this side of the fish you are going to catch. He won't move that far. Cast six inches farther at the same angle."

I stripped a couple of feet of line off my reel and started to cast. Jon

The Bighorn rainbow trout was right where Jon Madsen said it was.

stopped me. "Six inches, not two feet. If you cast that far, the leader will run right over his head. Take that line back in and start over."

After a two or three casts so Jon could read the length of my cast and the lie of the trout, he repeated, "OK, now cast six inches farther, same angle."

When my flies landed on the water, Jon said, "Good. You'll catch him on this cast. Now. There he is."

No need for me to set the hook! A 20 inch rainbow trout headed for the far bank, stripping line and scorching fingers. Sixty feet away the fish leapt clear of the water. Gradually, I regained line and brought the rainbow near. Jon netted it, we took a couple of quick pictures and released the fish. Twenty minutes into the trip and I already had a bragging size Bighorn rainbow.

"Bill," Jon yelled. "Come up here. Now it's your turn. There are more fish here. We'll catch you one."

As Bill made his way toward us, Jon instructed me to fish at the head of the riffle while Bill caught one. I could hear Jon instructing Bill he could see a trout at just such-and-such a spot and to cast in just such-and-such a way. Just as he had coached me.

After a couple of casts, Bill yelled, "I've got him!" Bill's fish ran diagonally upstream and jumped nearly at the far bank. From the color of Bill's line, I could tell the fish was into the backing. After a couple more leaps and runs, Bill seemed to have the fish under control. Jon was telling Bill how to bring the fish to the net. At the penultimate moment, the fish dove into the rocks and came loose.

We had been fishing half an hour, caught one and lost one. Both were quality fish Jon had seen in the running water and instructed us how and where to cast to hook them.

Maybe this guy really did see trout in the water. In fact, as the day wore on and on other days fishing with Jon, not only did he see feeding rainbows in the Bighorn riffles, he could teach us to see them as well.

For one thing, not all the riffles we saw held trout. Some spots Jon merely slowed the boat, scanned the water and said, "They're not here right now." At other riffles, Jon pulled the boat on the bank and suggested we fish a few minutes because fish would be coming onto the riffle shortly – and he was usually right. At some he hustled us out of the boat and into the water because rainbows were already in sight.

A common denominator among the riffles where Jon anticipated we would find feeding rainbows was all were upstream of a deep hole or pool. Once we got the hang of Jon's method, we could see individual fish moving over the ledge onto the riffle to feed. Indeed, Jon instructed us not to cast to trout moving into position to take nymphs we dislodged with our waders. "No fishing in the chum line," he instructed. To my amazement, I sometimes had substantial rainbows scarfing up bugs a few feet from my waders.

At one of the riffles, Jon left me to work a trout – a big fish – a dozen feet from the bank while he took Bill downstream. The gradient was pretty steep and only a perfect cast would get the flies to the feeding fish. I could see the trout, holding in the current, then darting out to grab something, then return to its lie. Gradually adjusting my casts, I hit the right angle and depth. The rainbow took my fly and headed downstream. By the time I yelled, "I've got him!" the trout already passed Jon and Bill and rapidly disappeared into the large pool. Gone. When a big trout had both his strength and the current working for him, that's all she wrote. I could not hustle down the bank fast enough to compete.

Releasing a Bighorn rainbow trout.

Typically we worked water less than four feet deep. As the depth of the riffles we fished varied, Jon adjusted the weight on our leaders. He carried a small amount of lead paste on the lens of his watch. If he wanted a little more weight, he scraped a bit off his watch and added it to our split shot. His adjustments were certainly more finely drawn any of mine. Of course, over time, the lead paste so obscured the face of Jon's watch he had only a vague idea of the time.

Sometimes he adjusted the length of leader between flies and strike indicator. Generally, he had us fishing with a strike indicator twice the distance from the flies as the depth of water he wanted us to fish.

If the sun went behind a cloud, not even Jon could see the trout. In our debriefing sessions in the evening, Bill and I recalled that on each of the riffles where we caught rainbows we had seen, Jon stationed us so the sunlight came from overhead or behind us. The trout were looking into the sun. We were not.

Polarized glasses. A must. Bill and I both had prescription polarized lenses. We did not have multiple hues of lenses for cloudy days, sunny days, and the variety of possible light conditions; perhaps we should. But drugstore sunglasses were not up to the task.

There were some tricks to knowing what we were seeing. Bighorn rainbows in rushing riffles were not as obviously trout as those you may see in modern aquaria. On the stream we were looking down on the fish, so the portion of them we saw was dark. Counter-shading, dark on the top and light on the bottom, is a major defense mechanism of animals with examples as diverse as whitetail deer and trout. Thus, every elongated form in the water could have been a trout. Could also have been a rock. But the rocks did not move. If we noticed a rock in the water, looked away, looked back and the rock was gone – that was a trout.

Nor did rocks suddenly flash white and then return to a stationary dark color. The white flash was the underbelly of a trout as it rolled to take some poor critter drifting down the stream. It was this sort of white flash Jon saw when he assured me I was going to catch the first of the day. The white might also be the inside of a trout's mouth, particularly if the fish was a little downstream, as it captured something good to eat.

Often a trout could be discerned, even if not actually seen. Perhaps there was a dark shadow over a clear bottom. The shadow was not the trout. The trout might be several feet from what we saw on the bottom, just as the shadow of a building may be a long way from the building itself. Depends on the angle which the sun hits the water. Early and late in the day, the shadow was farther from the position of the trout than at mid-day.

Jon instructed us, "Things in the water are not where you think they are. You have to cast the fly where it will come to the trout, not where the trout appears to be." When light passes from air to water, it bends. Physicists call this refraction. While different length light rays are refracted at different rates, what an angler really needs to know is that fish are a little shallower and closer than they appear. Adjust the depth and length of the cast accordingly. Jon's wisdom allowed him to modify the length of our casts so our flies drifted where the trout were, not where they appeared to be.

While the rainbows that moved out of the deeper pools were aggressive and feeding, they nonetheless sought locations in classic feeding lanes. Slightly deeper depressions between weeds or downstream from rocks, Bill and I learned, were prime locations. We had to examine them carefully.

Stand still! Pretty tough to make out a movement or trout in rushing water if we were moving too. And concentrate. The problems of the world will have to wait. Nothing you can do about them now anyway. (Turn off your cell phone.)

To get the hang of Jon's method, practice and more practice was the key. Once you learn how to see trout in a clear riffle, it gets easier and easier. Of course, a little quality instruction, as Bill and I had, helps as well.

We used pretty standard gear for the two nymph and strike indicator method. Our rods were 9 foot, 4 weights. We started with 9 foot leaders, tapered to 3X or 4X and added droppers as appropriate.

While we used several of the most common nymph patterns, many Bighorn trout were caught on a nondescript fly, we fished sizes 16 through 20, called a Ray Charles. The Bighorn is the only place I have seen this fly, but shops there are filled with them.

Jon was right and I was wrong. We could see trout in the turbulent water of the Bighorn riffles. Even ancient anglers like me could learn to do it. At one of the riffles where we stopped, Jon and Bill moved away as Bill battled a trophy rainbow. As they moved off, I studied the riffle. A rock appeared where none had been before. The rock moved, then moved back to the original spot. Gradually, I stripped line, adjusting my cast as Jon had taught. When my flies reached the precise spot, I had him!

Sight fishing in the Bighorn taught – at least new to me – a new and exciting way to catch trout. It gave me a new perspective on fishing riffles. Given the size and number of Bighorn rainbows Bill and I caught, I told Bill, "Custer would have been better off if he brought his flyrod."

Chapter 25
Lake Superior Lake Trout

In the early 1950's, when I first began trips to Grand Marais, Michigan, lake trout fishing in Lake Superior was one of the main attractions. Half a dozen or more charter captains fished for lakers. Many evenings my family visited the landing as the boats returned to display the fish caught. A small boy, I had no way to charter a trip. But I eyed the huge fish and envied those who caught them.

As many know, with the introduction of the lamprey eel in the late 1930s, lake trout fishing in Lake Superior suffered. By the 1950s the lamprey was taking its toll on Lake Superior lake trout fishing. And with it, the decline of Grand Marais. From the time when I first visited Grand Marais, when it had a couple of grocery stores, an ice cream shop, a hardware, by the 1970s the small town had taken a turn for the worse.

For those of a literary bent, the descriptions of Grand Marais in the novels of Jim Harrison, for example *True North* and *Returning to Earth,* are on the spot. When I first read those works, I thought to myself, "Damn, I wish I could write like that, capture the essence of a place so well."

Yet, times have changed. Grand Marais has come back. Dennis Weaver is a key figure in the rebirth. Dennis is a retired Marine Corps officer. He opened Grand Marais Outfitters on the main corner in town. He caters to hikers, campers, anglers, hunters – the outdoor enthusiasts who are the heart of Michigan's tourist industry. Shortly after he opened his shop a few years ago, I went in and introduced myself. In the intervening years, Dennis and I have stayed in touch. But he could not have done it without the lake trout.

A few days ago, when I went in to the shop to say "hello," Dennis said, "Let's go fishing." He fiddled with the computer on the counter and said,

"Weather's nice on Thursday. We'll go lake trout fishing." Who am I to complain?

We rendezvoused at the Grand Marais Marina about noon. Shane Buggs and Dale Ross joined us. Dennis took us several miles to a shoal off the Grand Sable Dunes.

When Dennis gave the signal, Dale and Shane rigged up and began to fish. We had been over 400 feet of water and came upon a shoal roughly 200 feet deep. Dennis explained, "We're going to maintain speed at close to 1.8 miles per hour. Experience shows, that's the optimal speed." To do that, of course, you need a depth finder that records not only depth but speed. Dennis called out depths frequently so Shane and Dale could adjust as needed.

Dennis said, "The lakers are close to the bottom. We see some suspended fish on the electronics but they rarely hit." Lures were kept close to the bottom with Cannon Downriggers.

Shortly after we started fishing, Shane hooked up. And landed a nice

Lake Superior lake trout, caught deeper than I had ever fished before.

Lake Superior lake trout. I took a couple of "grip and grin" photos and said, "I can go home now. I've got what I needed." Nobody laughed.

We talked about the colors which seemed to attract lakers. Dennis said, "Everybody has a favorite. But at 200 feet plus, there's not a lot of light penetration, I suspect it's a little bit of movement and light flash. I like spoons with a light color and a dark color on the same lure."

Dennis said, "On the depth finder, we're looking for some bait. A cluster. Probably herring or sticklehead." As we dressed our catch, one of the trout had a burbot about 10 inches long in its throat.

On the downriggers, Dennis and his buddies set the release from the cannonball as, what they called, "Pretty stiff." At 200 feet or more of line out, resetting the rig takes significant effort. If the tension on the release is too slight, every time the spoon hits the bottom, it releases. When it does, the whole system has to be pulled up and reset.

There's a flip side to that as well. Once a laker hits, the line has to be snapped from the release behind the cannonball. Secret is, point the rod tip at the line coming from the water and jerk, hard. It took me several efforts and good coaching from Dale and Shane to get the hang of it. Understand, from my perspective, 15 feet is deep water. Two hundred plus is a whole new ballgame.

And the rods were not what I expected. When Dennis asked me to go, I said I left my musky/pike gear behind. He said. "I have the rods." My gear would not have been appropriate. The rods were Shakespeare Ugly Stiks, 9 foot, with lots of flexibility. And all reels had counters to measure the line out.

Dale explained, "With the flexible rod, when a strike comes and the line pulls off the cannonball release, there may be lots of slack in the line. The big bend in the rod helps take up the slack before you can start reeling in."

I noticed, after the first fish was caught and dropped in the cooler, Dale, surreptitiously perhaps, stuck his hand in the cooler, and wiped it on his spoon. So I asked, "Dale, I saw you wipe some water from the cooler where the previously caught lake trout were on your spoon. You really think that makes a difference?"

Dale is an honest and decent man. He said, "I watched my kid do it and he told me…It's probably an old wives' tale."

Shane owns the grocery store in Grand Marais. And Dale works for the Alger County Road Commission. They are among the young entrepreneurs making Grand Marais tick.

Dennis is not a guide. Though when I queried him, he said, "Sometimes when people offer to take me for a boat ride, I show them a waypoint or two." Tell Dennis I sent you.

Chapter 26
On Being an Outdoor Writer:
A Pseudo Interview with
The New York Times

Each Sunday, the *New York Times* publishes in the Book Review section an interview with a noted author. Most have or had fiction on the Best Seller roster. Since I have not had fiction on the Best Seller list, I'm unlikely to be interviewed. So, using mostly questions from the *Times* with some variation to suit the occasion, I'm going to interview myself.

What books are on your bedside table? My bedside table includes the floor close to the bed. The floor is where most of my magazines go before they are read. On the table, I'm finishing Thomas C. Grubb, *The Mind of the Trout*. It's an analysis of trout based on optimum foraging behavior. I've also got Edward O. Wilson, *The Meaning of Human Existence*. Wilson is a biologist at Harvard and I've read several of his books. Also in the stack is Paul Kerlinger, *How Birds Migrate*. Outdoor writers need to have a good grounding in biology and not just in the areas they write about most frequently. Baseball has been a life-long passion and Nancy, my wife, got Michael A. Humphrey, *Wizardry: Baseball's Greatest Fielders Revealed* for me.

What stirred your interest in books and writing? My interest in books goes back to the beginning. Before I could read for myself, Dad read aloud *Treasure Island* and *Huckleberry Finn*. I still remember the horror I felt when Blind Pew was run down on the bridge. When Craig was in the crib I read *Treasure Island* to him, but he did not care for *Huckleberry Finn*. In the intervening years, I've read those book multiple times each. That Dad thought books were important was a more significant matter than the subject of the readings. I learned a critical lesson from the librarian in the small Michigan town where I lived. The library was only open a few hours, a few days. Mom let me walk to the library on my own. No one would let a kid do that now. When I got there the librarian – a very old woman, must have been 40 – asked me what kinds of books I liked. I told her I read a book about Robin Hood and enjoyed it. She said the book is right over here and sometimes books are worth reading more than once, so I took it. A few years ago I was in a remainder shop and saw a paperback *Robin Hood* for 95 cents. I bought it and it had to be the same because I could anticipate some of the events. Books are worth reading more than once – at least some are.

How did you get started as an outdoor writer? What was your first publication? Kind of dumb luck, I guess. Game and Fish Publications sent a questionnaire to subscribers. It was a simple "check the box" instrument. I filled it out, turned it over and banged out a couple of paragraphs in evaluation of the magazine I got. And sent it in. A week or so later I got a phone call at the University from Ken Dunwoody, Publisher at Game and Fish Publications. Nancy said he did not call at the house, and I have no idea how he got my number. Ken thanked me for my comments and asked if I ever did any writing. I told him I did academic writing, but had never done any free-lance. It had always been in my mind, I told him, to be an outdoor writer, but I had never pursued it. A few days later, Aaron Pass, then Editor of *Carolina Game and Fish,* called. Aaron asked what my "home lake" was, where I thought I was most likely to catch largemouth bass. I told him Currituck Sound. Aaron told me to write an article, submit it, and he'd buy it if he liked it. Of course, I had to count the words by hand. I wrote the draft while in Minneapolis at an academic conference. Aaron liked it and it ran in *Carolina Game and Fish* in March, 1984.

Norman Maclean published *A River Runs Through It* late in life. Most of his career was as a University of Chicago Professor of Shakespeare. Does that tell you anything about writing as a career? Well, Maclean's wonderful little volume is not about fishing. Fishing is in it, but that's not what the book is about. It's about the same subject as Kinsela's *Field of Dreams* which is superficially about baseball. What Maclean's career tells me is to write well, you have to read well. Two of my favorite contemporary writers, Ivan Doig and Jim Harrison, both have advanced degrees in history and literature. *True North* by Jim Harrison features Michigan's Upper Peninsula, including several small towns I know very well. Harrison nails them. [Both Doig and Harrison died in 2016, a few months apart.]

You are having a dinner party. What three writers in the same genre you write in would you invite? Rather than a dinner party, I think we would do better with pancakes in some cabin in the woods. Real maple syrup. Izaak Walton wrote the classic *The Complete Angler*. I read and re-read that book. One of my favorite Walton tenets is an angler cannot lose a fish "for no man can lose what he never had." John Gierach would add a contemporary perspective. Gierach writes a column for each issue of *Fly Rod and Reel*. His columns are collected into books and I have most of them. Not usually thought of as an outdoor writer, I'd also include Thomas McGuane. McGuane writes fiction, but he also collected essays into *The Longest Silence: A Life in Fishing*. What do these authors have in common, besides fishing? They write about fishing as a mirror on life. The conversation would be about more than where-to, how-to. If I could add another, I'd toss in Robert Traver, author of *Anatomy of a Murder*. Traver, actually a retired Michigan Supreme Court Justice, wrote several books superficially about trout fishing in northern Michigan but really about the enduring issues of life.

How would you describe your best writing? Most of what I've written in the years since I published my first article in the early 1980s has been where-to, how-to. Where can I go to catch some fish and when I get there, how can I catch them? But my best writing, and I think this is true of most of us, is narrative. My narratives meet the standard Huck Finn said Mark Twain set in *Tom Sawyer*. Huck said Twain, "told the truth, mainly." That's what I do, I tell the truth, mainly. Several people have told me when they read about themselves, "That's really what happened." Larry Barden, a good friend who has appeared in a number of my pieces, has often asked how I got the quotations – did I have a notebook he never saw? Did I record somehow? Or did I just remember? My book, *Quetico Adventures,* is principally narrative style.

What books might we be surprised to find on your shelves? I read widely. One of the things I've tried to do since I retired is to restore, perhaps extend, my liberal arts education, a thrust I had to put aside when I taught. I've read some of the Russian novelists, *War and Peace* by Tolstoy, a couple of novels by Dostoevsky, though *The Brothers Karamazov* sits here unread. Craig, my son, got me an APP for my phone which plays audio books over the radio in the truck. I'm most of the way through Cervantes, *Don Quixote.* Lots of biology books. Sitting here is Richard Dawkins, *The Greatest Show on Earth* and a friend sent me Gary Parker, *Creation: Facts of Life: How Real Science Reveals the Hand of God.* While I'm not reading the professional literature anymore, I've always thought I could have passed the Ph. D. written exams in American political history. I've been reading biographies of presidents. I'm about half way through, though some presidents have had multiple readings.

What books encouraged you to become an outdoor writer? I don't know that books had much to do with it. When I was in high school, I devoured *Field and Stream, Outdoor Life,* and *Sports Afield.* It occurred to me a couple of years ago that my folks subscribed to the magazines so I would stay home and read rather than run with the crowd. It worked. When the family traveled, we often played "What's My Line?" based on the popular TV show. I could never last very long as I picked one of the fishing writers or a Detroit Tiger baseball player. Certainly one of the crucially important books was Ray Bergman's *Trout.* Once when I came off the North Fork of the AuSable River, Mom said, "The man who was fishing there and came up ahead of you – he looked just like the man on the back of that book." Was I fishing with Ray Bergman?

When you are asked how to become an outdoor writer, what do you tell them? Read well, write often. About five years after I began publishing outdoor articles, I got a phone call. A chap wanted to become a writer and asked how to submit an article. I told him whom to contact and to submit clean copy, no typos, no grammatical errors, no spelling errors. He answered, "I can't do that. That's why magazines have editors." I've used my answer many times since. I told him, "Well, look at it this way. It's Friday afternoon and the editor has two articles on the desk, yours and mine, and one space to put it in. The editor gets a phone call saying to remember to pick up Susie at soccer practice, stop at the store and get a quart of milk, and not be late because there is a dinner party in the evening. Which article do you think the editor will buy?"

Chapter 27
How to Make a Trout Laugh

You want to know how to make a trout laugh? Trout don't laugh, you say. Too anthropomorphic. But they do, and I can tell you how to make them laugh.

A few days ago I was fishing one of my favorite stretches of Rock Creek in southwest Montana. Lots of trout there, browns, rainbows, a few westslope cutthroat, lots of cuttbows – a cross between the native cutthroat and the introduced rainbows. Over the years I've caught a bunch in the area.

You want to know my favorite spot? No way. OK, I'll tell you, it's between Gilles Bridge and Interstate 90. The Forest Service Road will be on the left of the stream. That should narrow it down some.

My first stop was at a 100 yard riffle, downstream from the other spot. Good dry fly section. It was not too swift for dry flies as the gradient was perhaps 1%. George M. LaBranch, when he wrote *The Dry Fly and Fast Water*, was thinking of the Catskill streams in contrast to the streams of the British Isles. His notion of fast water was not addressing the swift water of the mountain west of the United States. This section is not pocket water, really. But, as you might have guessed at Rock Creek, the bottom was covered with softball-sized stones with some basketballs in the mix. Deepest spots were three or four feet. The prime lies were readily apparent to any angler.

As my dry fly, I tied on a #14 parachute Adams. An Adams has always been a good choice and not just because it was created on the Boardman River, not far from where I was born. A little brown, a little gray, a little black. Looks buggy. On a dropper, I tied a #16 Beadhead Gold-ribbed Hare's Ear. Another buggy looking fly, but I'm not sure it "matches the

Fishing Rock Creek, knowing the trout are down there laughing.

hatch" of anything in particular.

Good start. On an early cast, a trout came to the Adams, splashed at it, and I missed the strike. Probably a little one. They do the little splash bit. Then nothing. I fished another half an hour with no action. Leon Sagaloff, a good friend and long-time trout guide, would have changed flies by now. If Leon was sure there were fish to be caught and nothing happened in 15 minutes, plus or minus, Leon changed flies. He did not want those guys sitting on the bottom making fun of his clients.

So, I changed to a Royal Coachman Trude as my dry fly. The Adams was not very colorful and the Royal Coachman was a "noisy" selection. A contrast. I fished the rest of the riffle. Did not get a strike. Near the far bank, however, I saw several trout take something off the surface. Perhaps they were just having fun at my expense.

So I went to what Uncle Bill Yunk, who was a dry fly purist, would think was the "dark side." I dug a Thingamabob® out of my sack and went to the popular two nymphs, strike indicator, and weights rig. I stuck with the Gold-ribbed Hare's Ear as one of my nymphs and added a #18 Copper

John as the second.

Then I discovered I dropped my point-and-shoot underwater camera. So I laid my rod in the tall grass and backtracked. In fact, I went back-and-forth over covered ground several times, all to no avail. I was going to show you pictures of all the trout I caught. Perhaps that's what happened to the camera.* The trout were shy and did not want to appear on Face-book.

Back to fishing. My rig was not bumping the bottom as it should, so I added weight. Now I had three split shot. Still not deep enough. So I ran more leader through the strike indicator. I was fishing another long riffle, but this one had a distinctive fast water, slow water seam where the water was four feet deep. I knew they were in there. With the rock-strewn bottom and seam, they had to be there, watching my flies drift by. They've been there before, they had to be there now.

OK. I'm not as good a trout angler as Chris Hunt. But come on.

Up to a long, deep pool. When Craig, my son, came to Montana to fish, I put him on this pool and went upstream to allow Craig space. I started to catch lots of fish. I thought I should go get Craig and put him on my spot, but I didn't. When we rendezvoused to leave for Butte, I apologized for leaving him on his own. He said, "Oh, no Dad. I caught 17 between 9:00 and noon. Those big cuttbows really are fun."

This time, I ran my double nymph rig close to the bottom for an hour. Close to the near bank. Close to the far bank. Along all the seams in the middle of the stream. At intervals, one or another trout rose to take something from or near the surface. They were there. Cast. Upstream mend. On one drift, the indicator dipped. I lifted the rod. Bingo. Brief struggle and I netted a seven inch Rocky Mountain whitefish. Bummer. You know the trout who saw the whitefish take the fly got a chuckle from watching their stupid cousin.

Trout had to be moving aside to let my flies drift through without snagging one of them. I've seen them do that. Six or seven trout in a pool, all facing into the current. Flies drifted with the current right to them. Some moved to the right. Some moved to the left. After the flies drifted through the opening, the trout resumed their previous position chuckling at the angler's expense. Today, in this pool, nothing.

OK, I'm not as good a trout angler as Squeak Smith. But come on.

Lunch break and time to think through my options.

Back to the last spot I fished. As I walked through the meadow between lunch and the stream, grasshoppers skipped away. Ah ha! Tie on a hopper.

When I got streamside, I propped my rod against the bushes and began to dig through my fly box. The terrestrial dry fly box was filled with more flies than I can ever use, the same as all my other boxes. Among them, I selected a foam-bodied fly, about a #10. A mixture of orange and brown, with rubber legs. I think this guy is called a Club Sandwich. No fan of the Catskill design would deign to use such a fly. As I tied it on, I turned away so the spirit of Dick Jones could not see me.

I took a few steps toward the stream, stripped six or seven feet of line from the reel and cast it. Before I could pull more line from the reel, the hopper disappeared in a strike. A fish in a foot of water and ten feet from my waders. So, the hopper was the answer. Shucks, a seven inch trout. But it was a westslope cutthroat, a rarity to catch one, so that was a positive.

No doubt, I found the key. Yet, as I made my way, I had a sinking feeling in my gut. The little cutthroat was down there being ridiculed by his peers for playing a sucker to my hopper. I worked upstream, fishing the seams. Casting to the far bank where even now trout periodically rose to something. Nothing on the hopper.

Gradually, I worked upstream. Around several fallen logs. Then to a long run, several feet deep across the entire stream, and the bottom made up of varied sized rocks. Ideal trout habitat and a run where I have caught many rainbows, browns and cutthroats over the years I've fished Rock Creek.

Carefully, I worked, step at a time, upstream. Floating the hopper in all the likely spots. Good drifts, one after another. Nothing doing. Yet, one rose there. One rose over there. One rose near the bank where I just cast. Nothing. Day's end.

OK, I'm not as good a trout angler as Kirk Otey. But come on.

Wiser folks than I tell me not to anthropomorphize, but I know trout on Rock Creek were laughing at me. I can feel it in my bones. And that's not imaginary.

*Later I found the camera. It dropped into my waders. But I did not need it to take pictures of fish anyway.

Alone, but not lonely in Quetico Park.

Chapter 28
Alone, But Not Lonely

In early 2016, I looked at the calendar. It said I was 78 years old. When I searched a 2017 calendar, the message was even worse. I was not going to be younger.

In the 30 plus years I have been visiting Quetico Park, I have often seen solo travelers. And I always admired them. I identified with them, though I had never made a solo trip. Sure, periodically I hiked into the North Carolina mountains alone and made overnight camping trips there. But never a multi-day, wilderness excursion.

Looking at all the other things which had to be done in 2016, I settled on early September as the time to make my solo trip. In late 2015, I purchased a Hobie Mirage Outback kayak. As things turned out, after I got it I only used it once. I resolved it, 12 foot long, would be my mode of travel in the Park. The kayak is heavy, 85 pounds. And there was no yoke making a portage convenient. That's OK. I simply put in at Prairie Portage and travelled up and down Basswood Lake. There were multiple options for camping and fishing I have never explored within a one day paddle of Prairie Portage. I named the kayak Rocinante, a carrier of adventurous old men.

RABC permit, check. Ontario fishing license, check. Reservations with an outfitter the night before entering the Park, check. Camping gear, check. One important change to my camping gear was a one burner stove. I would cook all my meals on this stove. No open fires. No scrounging firewood. No cursing trying to get a decent fire with wet wood.

Day 1

I got a tow to Prairie Portage. Truth be told, it was really not a tow. The kayak was lashed to a frame on a john boat and it, my gear and I were all whisked to the Canadian border. A couple of guys checked in at the Ranger Station ahead of me. When I spoke to the Ranger, I asked if, "Given those guys ahead of me, is today Geezer Day at Prairie Portage?"

She answered, "No, not particularly. It just happens." She and her coworker agreed, after the first of September, not many people were around. This was the first time in many years when Kathy was not on hand to check me in. A few years ago an article appeared, I think in *Field and Stream*, asserting the imperious conduct of a blonde Ranger at Prairie Portage. A few months after the article appeared as I checked in at the Ranger Station, Kathy asked me if I had seen it. She was obviously insulted, and she should have been. I told her the writer, if he did not like the rules in the Park, should have "stayed in New Jersey."

For many years I have passed by Little Merriam Bay, but never explored it. I pointed Rocinante in that direction. I paddled along the shore, looking for a suitable campsite. When I found none, I headed back toward Rookery Island and the small island just beyond it. With Hank Oates, I had camped there a number of years ago. Before I got that far, however, I found a nice site on a small island. One of the advantages of solo is, I did not have to camp where I planned to. I could change my mind without having to explain, maybe justify, a new tack.

By early afternoon, I was set up. Tent, tarp in case of pending rain, all in order and shipshape.

Heavy wind was coming out of the southwest. There were whitecaps heading my way from the direction of Ottawa Island. No time for my fly rod today. I paddled across to the protected side of Rookery Island and fished up toward the north end and back. As is true of everywhere I have fished Basswood Lake, smallmouth bass abound. But they were finicky today.

In the last decade, my "go to" smallmouth lure has been a tube grub. In the fall, I usually relied on somewhat larger offerings, so I tied on a three inch grub. Hit after hit after hit. But they kept coming off as they neared Rocinante. I trimmed a bit of the chartreuse tail to make the rig shorter and my hookup ratio improved. Yet, I could see these fish as they got close. They were hanging on to the tail, not taking the grub well enough to allow a good hookset. How many did I actually catch? I don't know – half a dozen or so. An advantage of being an old guy fishing alone is, it really didn't matter.

For a dozen years, I have prepared my own dried meals. Nancy, my wife of 50 plus years, suffered from high blood pressure. No salt diet. Commercially prepared freeze-dried offerings contain lots of salt. Accustomed to no salt, I can't eat those meals. So tonight, my own shrimp creole.

Post prandial, I made another cup of coffee, got the seat out of Rocinante, and watched the sun disappear beyond Canadian Point. Nobody asked me what we are going to do tomorrow, nobody asked me if I knew what bird made that call, nobody asked me whose turn it was to do the dishes. The dishes were already washed. I was just sitting, contemplating great thoughts. And sunset is a great thought.

Day 2

Breakfast. First, a couple cups of coffee. Those who have travelled with me know, I'm an addict. But today, I did not have to hustle in order to break camp and head for the next site. Indeed, the wind was still out of the southwest at a brisk clip. If I didn't want to, I didn't have to move at all.

Today, a staple of wilderness camping – instant oatmeal. I spruced mine up with flakes of dried apple I prepared at home.

Mid-morning, I loaded fishing gear, some snacks for lunch, and head-ed for Little Merriam Bay. Wind pushed me across the mile or so toward Salchert Island in the center of the bay. If the wind held, it was going to require a tough paddle to return to camp. But the island would block the wind from a major segment of the bay.

Hits immediately as I drifted and paddled along the shoreline. But they were still merely grabbing the tip of my grub, swimming around with it and letting go when they got close. I could see them release the tube. Yet, I landed six or seven along the northwest side of the island.

Salchert Island is a little less than a mile long and marked by several sizable points and bays. On one of the points there was a nice campsite. When I was checking for a place to stay yesterday, I did not check the island – solo, only me to blame. Subsequently, I located two more suitable sites on Salchert.

After I reached the northeast tip of the island, I paddled north to the shore of Little Merriam Bay. It, too, was reasonably protected from the blast from the southwest. More smallmouth bass, some hanging on and some dropping off. But steady action letting me know there were fish around. Suddenly, about a dozen feet from Rocinante, a huge swirl and bang. I had a big pike – maybe a dozen pounds. And this fish was hooked in the upper lip, no likelihood of the fish's teeth cutting the line. I was using the four-piece bait casting rod I purchased to accommodate trips where space, weight, and damage to equipment was an issue. This is a pretty nice bit of gear, but light to handle a fish like this. Three times she cleared the water, once so near water splashed on my lap. When the pike was sufficiently subdued, I reached down, twisted the grub with the bar-bless hook, and she drifted away. This was the biggest pike I've caught in Quetico for a number of years.

Late in the afternoon now. It was going to be a tough paddle home and no one was there to make dinner. As I passed the southwest tip of the island, I was heading directly into the wind. The fetch was about two miles and rollers a couple of feet high met me head on. Several times Rocinante took water over the bow. Yet, she remained stable in the water and I always felt secure.

In passing, the last several years I have always worn a PFD (personal floatation device, that's US Coast Guard terminology for a life vest). I bought a "paddler's" vest, with large arm holes to facilitate paddle or oar manipulation. In a canoe or kayak, I do not wear a unit activated by contact with water. A wave splashing on it could render it useless when it was needed. Is use of the PFD an accommodation to getting older? Or just late-onset wisdom?

Something I had never seen before. Perhaps 150 feet from the island where I was camped, 50 or more herring gulls and at least eight loons were in a compact cluster. Gulls rose from the water, swooped down, then landed. Loons dove and popped right back up. Some sort of forage fish were being driven to the surface by predator fish – lake trout? smallmouth bass? The part I had never seen before was the mingling of loons and gulls. Had it not been for the wind and the distance I would lose if I stopped paddling, I would have made a couple of casts to find out what species was pushing the prey to their doom. As it was, I paddled through the birds and they paid little attention to me, not flying off, not squawking, not diving to avoid Rocinante as she passed among them. The loons and the gulls – they kept me company.

The original setting of the tarp left it as a great sail, billowing and snapping in the wind. I reoriented it to let the wind pass under it and lowered it as well. Looked like rain.

My original plan had been to keep moving camp to explore new areas. Too much wind. This was a cozy spot. I stayed put.

Once in the tent, I was disturbed by thumping sounds outside. Took me a few minutes to figure out what caused the noise. White cedars were heavy with clumps of cones. Red squirrels harvested the clumps, cutting several at a time and letting them fall, then scurrying away with them to hoard for winter. My tent was near a huge white cedar and the squirrels were bombing me.

Day 3

It was still blowing, hard, from the southwest. Man, was it ever going to quit? Yet, nobody to satisfy but myself. A sort of cantankerous cuss, but nonetheless.

After a leisurely breakfast, I mounted Rocinante and ducked south of Rookery Island, past the campsite where I stayed with Hank Oates (note to Hank, a big red pine has fallen across the site), and fished the west bank of Big Merriam Bay. Lots of smallmouth, a couple of small pike. Three cast distances away from the bank, I noticed a swirl, then another. I laid to the paddles and when I was within reach, I threw my tube as far as I could. It scarcely hit the water when I had a strike. Three pound smallmouth. Then a smaller one. By the time I landed the second, they had moved to somewhere I did not know.

Something I have to master. With the kayak, on each stroke, water dripped off the paddle onto my lap. On the paddles there were rubber

Dinner for one, coming up in Quetico Park.

gaskets which slid toward the blade. The gaskets caught lots of the water. I suspected my troubles were related to the difference between a canoe paddle stroke and a kayak paddle stroke. I resolved to work on that.

After dinner, tonight elk jerky stew, I swished off my pants in the lake to clear off some accumulated mud. I draped my pants over a white pine, tied them to the tree and crawled in the tent. About 8:00 it began to rain. I started to get up and move my pants, but the rain stopped. Sometime later I realized it was raining hard. It rained hard well into the next day. It was too late now to rescue my pants.

Day 4

Late start today. Rained most of the night and into the morning. On my electronic book, I had *The King James Bible* and *The Complete Works of Charles Darwin*. One of the Rangers noted the juxtaposition of sources, but I had plenty to read for company.

Toward lunch time, I headed off to fish the southeast shore of Salchert Island. Lots like other parts of Little Merriam Bay. Caught two nice smallmouth and a six or seven pound pike on a topwater lure.

Wind was still hard out of the southwest. Another tough paddle back to camp.

Days 5 and 6

Reprise of the earlier three days. Strong wind from the southwest. One day I fished Big Merriam Bay and one day Little Merriam Day. Lots of water in Big Merriam Bay. Though my goal had been to explore it extensively, had I taken an easy paddle to the north end, wind would have made a tough return. So I stayed as close and as protected as I could.

Long about 8:00, after I was already tucked in, a nearby loon let out a lonely wail, saying to all the other loons, "I'm over here. Where are you?" He got dozens of answers. Which required dozens more. Soon a loon symphony lulled me to sleep.

Day 7

Moving day. In order to make an easy paddle out on the ninth day, I wanted to get closer to Prairie Portage. My original plan had been to camp somewhere a day or two, move somewhere else for a day or two. Explore lots of areas in Basswood Lake I never visited. But the severe wind every day discouraged me from loading Rocinante and relocating. But today was moving day.

By 9:00 I had broken camp, loaded the kayak, and started toward Sunday Island. For one thing, I knew several great campsites on the island. For another, there has always been great fishing in Sunday Bay.

Today, the wind helped. It pushed me past Norway Point and across Bayley Bay. Indeed, I had to correct course constantly as the wind wanted me to land at the portage into Burke Lake. Roughly noon, I was set up on a favorite site at the southeast corner of Sunday Island. Since I was there last, three huge white pines had fallen, taking several white cedars and other trees with them.

Further, folks had dismembered an excellent fire ring against a huge rock to assemble several smaller and less useful spots for cooking. Even worse, several folks had carved their names into logs around the original fire ring. Some, I guess, liked the wilderness but did not appreciate it.

Wind was creating havoc. Waves a couple of feet high. Langmuir Current in spades. But I ducked across a narrow spot and began to fish along the southeast corner of Sunday Bay. No fish, at least that I could interest, along the weedy bank. Eric Yarborough and I caught a bunch there a couple of years ago. I switched from the tube grub to a small minnow-like jerk bait. A hundred yards east of the portage to Sunday Lake, I hooked a huge (at least for northern standards) largemouth bass. Not the biggest largemouth I ever caught, or even caught this year. But by Quetico Park standards, a trophy. Five, maybe six pounds. She pulled Rocinante in circles. Released to spread her genes another spring.

Day 8

Wind was blowing out of the southwest, as it has the entire trip.

As I ducked around the corner of Sunday Island seeking calm water to fish, three canoes came by. We chatted briefly. When asked if I had been here before and I replied I thought this was my 28th or 29th trip, one chap said it was his 31st, but, "I live a lot closer." He and his companions debated what to do next, given the wind. They decided to head for the portage to Burke Lake, despite the wind, on the grounds it was easier than the portage into Sunday and, "We've already done the hard part." Off they went.

A few paddle strokes further, I saw a canoe pulled up to the bank. A chap wandered down to the water, asked if I was camped, "over there," and explained he and his partner were in no hurry and planned to wait out the wind.

I fished up the west shoreline of Sunday Bay. Steady action with typical Quetico Park smallmouth bass – maybe a couple of pounds, not much more. As I got toward the northwest corner of the Bay, I noticed lily pads in small clusters away from the shoreline. I began to cast the small jerkbait I used yesterday around the lily pads. And I began to catch larger smallmouth. Among them, one I guessed just shy of five pounds; and my camera battery went dead with the previous picture.

Shortly after I got back to camp, the chap waiting out the wind, came to my site. He asked, "Do you have a cell phone that works?" I said I did but it was in my truck. He allowed he asked a question he did not mean, chuckled a bit, and we talked a few minutes. As he got ready to leave, he turned and asked, "This is not something I usually do, but would you mind if my friend and I came over after dinner to talk?" I told him it was fine with me.

So, sure enough, Steve, the guy I had spoken with earlier, and Kevin came over to chat. In all my trips to Quetico, I have had many encounters with other travelers, but this was a first – a purely social visit. Good guys. We railed against injustice, stupidity, carelessness and other ills of the world.

Day 9

Out. Up fairly early. Camp broken. Rocinante loaded. Paddling toward Prairie Portage by shortly after 8:00. Calm. First day the wind was not stiff out of the southwest. About two and a half miles to Prairie Portage, then another eight to the outfitters. Easy paddle to Prairie Portage, took two hours and a few minutes.

I began to lug my gear across the portage. When I got to the end of the trail, there sat Steve and Kevin. Steve made some remark to the effect, "We thought you'd never get here. What have you been doing all morning?"

On my second trip across the portage, the young lady from the outfitters I had met the evening before I came into the Park was part way down the trail. She asked, "Are you my guys?"

I answered, "No," but I determined she was here to meet a party needing a tow. I asked if I could get on her tow if the other party agreed. And she said I could.

I started to drag Rocinante across the trail. And found it a tough go. I left her. Went to the end of the portage and asked Steve and Kevin, "Would one of you help me get my kayak?" Steve jumped up, helped me tote her to the tow boat.

Once back at the outfitter's I shared my business card with the two guys whose tow I jumped. One recalled the many articles I had done for *Boundary Waters Journal.*

Great trip and I had a wonderful time. The company was good, too. Finis.

Chapter 29
Why I Fish – One Angler's Perspective

"You must be miserable! I can't understand why you do that," Nancy, my wife, asserted as I came in the back door. Despite a 40 minute ride in a heated pickup truck, my clothes were still wet and I was chilled through.

Driving rain and late fall greeted me when I got to Lake Tillery. I knew I had a boat ride 10 miles to get to the spot I wanted to fish. But I went anyway. I answered her question, "No, I'm not miserable. I had a wonderful time. Big largemouth bass were chasing baitfish at the upper end of the lake. I must have caught 30 or 40. Sometimes big fish, four or five pounds, came toward my lure only to have a smaller one – a two or three pounder – dash in and grab it."

Nancy was often confronted with suppositions, "You must eat a lot of fish," and she answered with, "Oh, no. He lets them go." As a means of providing fish for the dinner table, angling as a sport is incredibly inefficient. Equipment, licenses, travel expenses, and the host of miscellaneous costs far exceed the value of fish caught.

Many folks think fishing is sitting on the river bank, lolling in the sun, cold beverages on hand, hoping nothing happens to disrupt an afternoon nap. Others know fishing seems to be done only when the weather is too hot or too cold, too wet or too dry, the insects are too thick and predatory, and the fish are not biting. All of these things may be true.

Not every trip is successful, at least as far as catching fish is concerned. In the 70 plus years I have been an angler, there have doubtless been as many trips when no fish were caught as when fish were (though I will claim, I've gotten better and trips with no fish are now quite rare).

Ted Trueblood, one of the heroes of my youth, long-time writer for *Field and Stream* and other magazines I devoured as they came in the mail, explained that about a quarter of what he carried in his tackle box was of spiritual value only. Banks Miller, a much better angler than I, once told me that at the end of the year he went through his tackle and each lure that did not catch a fish got discarded. I've never been able to do that. The spiritual value of lures that once caught fish or might on the next trip is too great.

Fishing has provided a binding together of generations. Dad taught me to fish. Then it was my turn to teach Craig, though he is now a grown man doing a good bit of the teaching himself. Golf, bridge, chess and a myriad of other activities can link generations. Fishing is not unique in that regard.

Dad took me fishing in northern Michigan, according to family legend, at the lake behind the house longer ago than I can remember. And I caught speckled bass (I learned later that in much of the country they are called crappie) until the minnows were all gone. Dad said he held onto the back of my life jacket and I cried when we had to go home.

Years later, living in northern Virginia, it was my turn. Craig was just past three years old. On a warm spring day, we fished for bluegills. Repeating Dad's experience, Craig fished and I and took off the wiggling panfish he caught, one after another. I knew Craig was paying attention when he told me I made a bad cast in his behalf. He said, "Daddy, it's got to be closer to that rock."

Among the most rewarding times fishing have been when Dad, Craig, and I fished together. When Craig was little, Currituck Sound in North Carolina was among the hot largemouth bass destinations in the country. We fished together there often. Rather, Dad and I fished and Craig did whatever. On one of the trips, Craig indulged his newly discovered ability to read with E. B. White's classic, *Charlotte's Web*. Though we were not keeping any, Craig also assigned himself the duty to net any fish we caught. He always leapt to duty when Dad or I yelled, "Fish on." A fat two or three pounder latched onto my lure and Dad alerted Craig, "Craig. Get the net. Your dad's got a fish." Craig did not move. Again, "Craig, get the net. Hurry up."

Craig stood up, still clutching his book. "I can't get the net now,

Grandpa. I have to finish this paragraph." We savor that exchange.

For years, Craig and I travelled to northern Michigan to fish for northern pike with Dad. We crammed ourselves into Dad's little aluminum boat and circled small lakes casting to weedbeds. When one of us caught a fish, we yelled and carried on like little kids. And for a few moments, we were.

For several years, Dad and I went to backcountry lakes in Canada pike fishing. Subsequently, Craig and I did. Unfortunately for all three of us, Dad's age and Craig's age did not overlap sufficiently to allow all three of us to go together. We would have had a great time.

In addition to Craig, I have enjoyed passing on angling to others. Perhaps none more than to Jack Murphy. Jack is the son of a former student. Neither of his parents fish, but somewhere Jack caught the bug. Wendy, Jack's mom, asked if I would take Jack fishing. We've been together a dozen or so times, though Jack lives far away and we do not get to go together as often as we would like. On one of our trips, Jack caught a big carp – I guessed it weighed 11 pounds. The *Charlotte Observer* published a picture of Jack grinning and holding the big fish. Jack became a celebrity to all his friends and cousins. Do you know how little is required to become a hero to a youngster? And how profound the satisfaction? The mystery is why everyone does not do it.

Many of my dearest friends have also come my way as a result of our fishing experiences. These few lines do not permit elaboration but include among them (in no order) Gordy Johnson, Clyde Osborne, Banks Miller, Tony Garitta, Mike Quinn, Tim McDermott, Bill Kraft, Bill Shumaker – doubtless I left some out.

A common theme of folks defending their interest in fishing is the beauty of places they fish. True, trout do not live in ugly places. At least, trout rarely live in ugly places. Yet, opening day of the trout season on Pennsylvania's Yellow Breeches down the hill from where we lived was always lined, rod tip to rod tip, with anglers seeking newly stocked trout. It was not a pleasant sight, for me anyway. From time to time, I've caught largemouth bass in North Carolina from shorelines with piles of old tires, abandoned refrigerators, and an abundant variety of trash. Many of the beautiful outdoor sights I've seen, however, have been on fishing trips – the mountains of Alaska. Wyoming, Montana, and North Carolina; the boreal forest scattered across North America. But if all I wanted was scenic beauty, I'd drop my fishing gear and grab my camera.

Robert Traver, the pen name of John Voelker who resigned from the Michigan Supreme Court after publishing *Anatomy of a Murder*, in a brief "Testament of a Fisherman," said he fished to avoid crowds, television, and cocktail parties. It appeared to Traver most persons spent their lives doing something they hate. (Thoreau claimed, in *Walden*, "Most men lead lives of quiet desperation.") That's why he left a post at the pinnacle of the legal profession to go fishing. And, fishing, Traver said, held out the hope "maybe one day I will catch a mermaid." I've never anticipated catching a mermaid and I'm not sure I'd know what to do if I did. Finally, Traver said, he fished, "…not because I regard fishing as being so terribly important but because I suspect that so many of the other concerns of men are equally unimportant – and not nearly so much fun."

Izaac Walton, author of The *Compleat Angler* published in 1653, captured many of the spiritual values of fishing. Among Walton's insights was that angling compares with mathematics as an activity never to be fully mastered but always offering more to learn.

There is always, at least for me, a new trick to learn, some new observation to make, a hypothesis to confirm or deny. Despite the careful teaching of experts like Dad, Craig, Ted Trueblood and other heroes of my youth – Ray Bergman of *Outdoor Life* and Jason Lucas of *Sports Afield* – I still need to learn more. After all these years, I still have not got it all figured out. If I am lucky, I never will.

Walton, perhaps as well as anyone has in 300 years, explained why I fish. He wrote, "…in ancient times a debate hath risen, and it remains yet unresolved whether the happiness of man in this world doth consist more in contemplation or action? …both these meet together, and do most properly belong to the most honest, ingenious, quiet, and harmless art of angling."

About the Author

Tim Mead began camping and fishing more than 70 years ago with his father in northern Michigan. In the intervening years, he has continually honed his outdoor skills and adventures into Ontario's Quetico Provincial Park have played a key role in his development as an outdoorsman. Mead's articles and photographs have appeared in a wide range of international, national and regional magazines. He is a Past President of the Southeastern Outdoor Press Association and a past member of the Board of Directors of the Outdoor Writers Association of America. Both organizations have recognized Mead's work with Excellence in Craft awards.

Quantity discounts are available to your company or nonprofit for resellng, educational purposes, subscription incentives, gifts and fundraising campaigns. For more information, please contact the publisher.

Ancient Angler Press
7124 Chaparall Ln.
Charlotte, NC 28215
www.TimMeadFishing.com
ancientanglertim@aol.com

CPSIA information can be obtained
at www.ICGtesting.com
Printed in the USA
FFOW03n0320110417
34418FF

9 780988 939417